Problem Solving
Current Issues
SECOND EDITION

Open Guides to Psychology

Series Editor: Judith Greene, Professor of Psychology at the Open University

Titles in the series

Learning to Use Statistical Tests in Psychology
Judith Greene and Manuela D'Oliveira

Basic Cognitive Processes
Judith Greene and Carolyn Hicks

Memory: Current Issues (Second Edition)
Gillian Cohen, George Kiss and Martin Le Voi

Language Understanding: A Cognitive Approach
Judith Greene

Problem Solving: Current Issues (Second Edition)
Hank Kahney

Perception and Representation: A Cognitive Approach
Ilona Roth and John Frisby

Designing and Reporting Experiments
Peter Harris

Biological Foundations of Behaviour
Frederick Toates

Running Applied Psychology Experiments
John Leach

Problem Solving
Current Issues
SECOND EDITION

Hank Kahney

Open University Press
Buckingham · Philadelphia

Open University Press
Celtic Court
22 Ballmoor
Buckingham
MK18 1XW

and
1900 Frost Road, Suite 101
Bristol, PA 19007, USA

In association with The Open University

First published 1986 as *Problem Solving: A Cognitive Approach*
Second edition first published 1993

ISBN 0 335 19080 4

A CIP catalogue record for this book is available from the British Library.

Library of Congress Cataloguing Publication Data is available.

Edited and designed by The Open University
Typeset by Graphicraft Typesetters Limited, Hong Kong
Printed in Great Britain by Biddles Limited, Guildford and Kings Lynn

*This book is dedicated to Eric, Leander, Alexander,
Christopher, Chloe, Tabetha, and Josh*

Problem Solving

Contents

Preface

Within the Open Guides to Psychology series *Problem Solving* is one of a companion set of four books, the others being *Language Understanding*, *Memory*, and *Perception and Representation*. Together these form the main texts of the Open University third level course in Cognitive Psychology, but each of the four volumes can be read independently. The course is designed for second or third year students. It is presented in the style and format that the Open University has found to be uniquely effective in making the material intelligible and interesting.

The books provide an up-to-date, in-depth treatment of some of the major issues, theories and findings in cognitive psychology. They are designed to introduce a representative selection of different research methods, and the reader is encouraged, by means of Activities and Self-assessment Questions (SAQs) interpolated through the text, to become involved in cognitive psychology as an active participant.

The author gratefully acknowledges the many helpful comments and suggestions of fellow members of the course team and of the external assessor Michael W. Eysenck on earlier drafts, and the valuable assistance of Pat Vasiliou in typing the manuscript.

Acknowledgements

Grateful acknowledgement is made to the following for material used in this book:

Figures
Figures 1.12 and 1.13: based on Kotovsky, K., Hayes, J.R. and Simon, H.A. (1985) 'Why are some problems hard? Evidence from the Tower of Hanoi', *Cognitive Psychology*, 17, pp.248–94, reproduced by permission of Academic Press Inc.; *Figure 2.1:* based on Figure 1 in Chase, W.G. and Simon, H.A. (1973) 'Perception in chess', *Cognitive Psychology*, 4, pp.55–81, reproduced by permission of Academic Press Inc.

Tables
Table 2.4: adapted from Table 5 in Gick, M.L. and Holyoak, K.J. (1980) 'Analogical problem solving', *Cognitive Psychology*, 12, pp.306–55, reproduced by permission of Academic Press Inc.; *Table 3.10:* Pellegrino, J.W. and Glaser, R. (1982) 'Analyzing aptitudes for learning: inductive reasoning', in R. Glaser (ed.) *Advances in Instructional Psychology* (vol. 2), Lawrence Erlbaum Associates.

Introduction

This book is divided into three parts. Part I discusses early research on problem solving by cognitive psychologists. The aim is to introduce you to some of the tools that were developed during this period for carrying out problem-solving research. Part I introduces one of the main themes of the book, which concerns the effects of experience in learning and problem solving. Part I also presents a very influential theory of human problem solving, devised by H.A. Simon, which depicts man as an active processor of information. Parts II and III discuss modifications or elaborations of Simon's information-processing model, exploring the role and limits of cognitive representations and processes in learning to solve problems.

In Part II we turn again to questions about the role of previous experience in problem solving. Here we shall consider some of the mechanisms that psychologists have suggested are involved in identifying and utilizing past experience in solving new problems. Part II also considers recent research on problem solving by novices and experts in various domains of knowledge, and computer implementations of the types of processes involved in problem solving and learning.

Part III considers recent research on 'intelligence' by cognitive psychologists. We discuss the processes underlying behaviour on a subset of intelligence test tasks, and explore the question of whether or not intelligence can be 'trained'. Of particular importance is the question of whether or not training on particular intelligence test tasks generalizes to different situations, such as performance in the classroom.

There are, however, topics of major interest to psychologists interested in thinking and learning that are not covered in this book. The major omissions are studies of rational and irrational reasoning processes. There is a huge literature on the topic of logical reasoning and I recommend the following books as good introductions to these areas of research. First, there is Richard E. Mayer's text on problem solving called *Thinking, Problem Solving, Cognition*, published by W.H. Freeman, 1983. This text not only discusses research on deductive and inductive reasoning, but also provides a very good coverage of the historical roots of the cognitive approach to problem solving. There is a long section devoted to considering the applications and implications of the cognitive approach. A good introduction to issues in the study of human deductive and inductive reasoning, as well as a personal view of the nature of biases in reasoning by an eminent researcher in the field, is Jonathan St B.T. Evans's *Bias in Human Reasoning, Causes and Consequences*, published by Lawrence Erlbaum Associates, 1989. A third recommended text is John R. Anderson's *Cognitive Psychology and Its Implications* (3rd edn), published by W.H. Freeman, 1990. This book is more of a standard undergraduate psychology textbook, and gives good coverage of perception, memory, language and child development as well as problem solving. Finally, a very good review of research on analogical reasoning in children is provided in U. Goswami's *Analogical Reasoning in Children*, published by Lawrence Erlbaum Associates, 1992.

How to use this guide

Throughout this book you will find a number of Self-assessment Questions (SAQs) and Activities. These have been designed to help you become an active participant in understanding and applying the concepts presented in the text. Attempting all of the SAQs will help you to assess what you have and have not understood in the preceding sections, and will also provide you with an opportunity to organize what you have learned. The Activities often present you with an opportunity to experience for yourself the kind of difficulties experimental subjects have when they tackle particular problems, and the problems confronting a psychologist who wants to understand what is going on when people solve some kind of problem. You will find the answers to the SAQs at the end of the book.

The book also contains a number of Techniques Boxes which describe various experimental techniques that have been used by psychologists in studying learning and problem solving. Each main section of the book ends with a Summary which highlights the main points that have been made. There is an Index of Concepts at the end of the book which indicates the page on which a concept is first introduced and defined.

Part I
Introduction to
Problem Solving

Contents

1 Introduction

Here is a list of problems. Some of them you will recognize as familiar, reflecting the concerns of most people in our culture, while others will be problems with which you are unconcerned yourself, but which you would recognize as problems for certain other people. Some of the problems you may never have heard of, even though they are probably the simplest of all the problems in the list.

How do you write the Great American Novel?
How am I going to pay this bill?
What's the best way to avoid tomorrow's predicted traffic jam?
How am I going to pass this examination?
How do I beat this guy at Nim?
What does 'anaphoric' mean?
Where's that Phillips screwdriver?
How can I get out of that appointment on Thursday so I can go to see the Rolling Stones?
How can I divide the water in the first jug between that jug and a second jug using only the three jugs provided?
How can you draw four straight lines through a three-by-three array of nine dots without taking your pen off the paper?
How can I avoid person X?
How can I attract person Y?
How can I motivate my children to make the most of their schooling?
Starting with three rings on one peg, how can I move all the rings to a third peg without breaking the rules?

All of the above problems have two things in common. First, they all specify a *goal*, whether it is paying a bill or knowing the meaning of an unfamiliar word. Secondly, in each case the solver is not immediately able to achieve the goal because the goal is blocked either through lack of resources or knowledge. These facts can be used as a basis for a definition of the concepts of *problem* and *problem solving*. Whenever you have a goal which is blocked for any reason — lack of resources, lack of information, and so on — you have a problem. Whatever you do in order to achieve your goal is problem solving.

Perhaps the most important aim of problem-solving research is the development of a theory of problem solving that explains the interactions between a problem situation and the person who is confronted by the problem. To paraphrase Greeno (1978), we would like to be able to say, 'Look, there are essentially five (or ten or fifteen or whatever) types of problem. Any problem you name can be categorized as one of these types, or some combination of them'. If we were able to categorize

15

problem types, we could devote our research efforts to understanding the strategies used by people who are successful at solving particular categories of problems. Once we knew that, we could revolutionize educational practice by teaching students successful strategies for solving all kinds of problems. That's the dream. But the development of a general theory of problem solving is a complex undertaking. Even the very small list of problems at the beginning of this Introduction indicates that the range of problems is vast. It would be difficult, too, for most people to say what any two of these problems have in common.

Given that we could categorize the structures of problems, the next question we would need to consider concerns the processes and strategies adopted by problem solvers. One research method involves studying a single type of problem in depth. One such problem type is known as a *transformation problem* (Greeno, 1978), because it involves moves which transform one situation into another. Various transformation problems will be introduced later, but you can get an intuitive feel for the type of problem by considering the task of mixing paints. If you want a light shade of grey, and you have some black paint and some white paint, you could pour a bit of black paint into the white and mix the paints together; that is, transform the state of the white paint by mixing it with black. The result is either the shade of grey you want to end up with or it is still the wrong shade. If it is correct, you stop. If not, you pour in some more black paint (or white, if it's now too dark a shade of grey) and mix again (second transformation). So transformation problems can be defined as problems that require 'moves' which transform one state (white) into another state (grey). Most of Part I of this book is devoted to a discussion of research on such problems, primarily because a great amount of research effort has been devoted to problems of this general type. Indeed, Simon (1978) points out that most of what we know about learning and problem solving was discovered by analysing the behaviour of people solving transformation problems.

Equally important, the problems are simple and interesting enough for you to do a considerable amount of research on your own, partly for the fun of it and partly for the experience of studying problem solving at first hand.

1.1   Getting started on problem solving

Activity 1 contains an example of a typical transformation problem — the *Towers of Hanoi problem*. Solving the problem involves moves which transform one state of the problem into another state. In Activity 1, the problem is presented in the way it is normally given. But there are also instructions on how to set up the problem using coins and paper for your own attempt at it. NB Taking time to do the Activities is well worth while. You will get a much better understanding of what problem solving involves and will probably find the experience enjoyable as well.

Activity 1
The Towers of Hanoi   Starting with three rings of different sizes — a small (SSS) ring, a medium-sized (MMMMM) ring, and a large (LLLLLLL) ring — on Peg A (see 'Initial situation' in Figure 1.1), your task is to move all of the rings to Peg B (as in the 'Goal situation' in Figure 1.1) in the fewest number of moves. Your solution is subject to the following constraints: (1) you can only move one ring at a time, and (2) you may not place any ring on top of a smaller ring. (And, of course, rings may only be placed on one of the three pegs, not placed on, for example, the table or floor.)

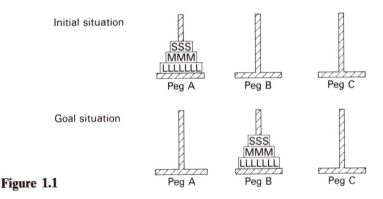

Figure 1.1

What I would like you to do is get out a tape recorder (if you have one) and 'think out loud' while you are solving the problem. Try to say everything you think about while you work on the problem. So, as you work on the problem you will be deciding what moves you should make. You will also have a reason for making the moves. You should describe both out loud and record them. You will be able to transcribe the tape (make a written record of its contents) at a later time. If you don't have access to a recorder, make a written record of the decisions you take in solving the problem and your reasons for them. This record is called a *protocol*.

In order to set up this problem, get out a piece of paper and draw three circles side by side, about two inches apart, and, starting from the circle on the left, label them 'Peg A', 'Peg B' and 'Peg C' respectively. Then place three different sized coins on 'Peg A', with the largest on the bottom and the smallest on the top. Finally, moving the coins one at a time and without ever placing a coin on top of a smaller one, transfer all the coins over to 'Peg B'.

SAQ 1
How many steps (moves) did you take in solving the problem? What is the minimum number of steps needed to solve the three-ring Towers of Hanoi problem?

You might find it incredible that researchers think they can learn anything about real-world problem solving by creating 'toy worlds' — puzzle-like tasks such as the Towers of Hanoi problem. However, there is nothing intrinsically wrong with studying simple, even contrived, phenomena. This is like engineers making small models for use in wind tunnels. All sciences create 'toy worlds' for close examination, mainly because the real world is very complex and messy. As psychologists we are interested in what we learn from studying toy worlds only to the extent that it helps us to understand how people behave in the real world, which is the actual focus of our interest.

Researchers have spoken of numerous advantages in using simple tasks in laboratory studies of problem solving. One advantage is that no prior special knowledge is necessary. People are given all the information they need in order to solve problems such as the Towers of Hanoi, so investigators do not have to worry about different people bringing different amounts of knowledge to the task. The Towers of Hanoi task itself involves discrete, observable stages; the processes involved in solving the problem are slow and easily verbalizable. Another advantage is that the same problem can be dressed up in different guises, and researchers can use this fact to ask questions about the effect of experience with one problem when a subject is confronted with a new problem having the same underlying structure. Still another advantage is that whole families of problems can be developed from one of the core problems. For example, the Towers of Hanoi problem can be made more difficult simply by adding to the number of rings that have to be moved from one peg to another. In this way we can look at the effect of experience on 'scaled up' problems — at the effect, say, of prior experience on the three-ring problem when confronted for the first time with the five-ring problem. In the real world, it's like asking if experience in designing and building a garden shed scales up to designing and building a house.

Finally, as Simon (1978) pointed out, real-world problems often take hours, days, perhaps even a working lifetime to solve (without any guarantee of success). On the other hand, even complex versions of the Towers of Hanoi problem (and others) can be solved by most people, usually in an hour or less. Because such relatively short solution times are involved, experimenters are able to shift attention from the question of whether or not people succeed in solving a problem to the question of *how* they solve it, or how quickly.

In the 'real world', transformation problems occur in domains such as logic, physics and mathematics, as well as in mixing paints and cocktails. If studies of toy-world problems really are pertinent to real-world concerns, then what we learn about problem solving in the simpler situations should help us to understand problem solving in the more complex situations. And indeed, cognitive psychologists have begun to test their ideas in the classrooms of schools and colleges. We shall take up this strand of the story in Part II.

1.2   Well-defined and ill-defined problems

One distinction often made between real-world problems and laboratory problems is how well they are defined. In a *well-defined problem*, that is, in a well-structured problem, the solver is provided with all the information needed in order to solve the problem. In well-defined problems the solver is provided with four different sorts of information:
1 information about the *initial state* of the problem;
2 information about the *goal state*;
3 information about *legal operators* (things you are allowed to do in solving the problem);
4 information about *operator restrictions* (factors which govern or constrain the application of operators).

We can illustrate the notion of a well-defined problem with reference to the Towers of Hanoi problem. Look back to the instructions in Activity 1 and re-read the problem statement. The information given is the following:
1 *Initial state.* In the Towers of Hanoi problem the initial state is the set of three different-sized rings piled up in a particular way on peg A, an empty peg, Peg B, to the right of Peg A, and another empty peg, Peg C, on the extreme right.
2 *Goal state.* The goal state is achieved when the set of different-sized rings are piled up on Peg B, with the small ring on top, the large ring on the bottom, and the medium-sized ring in the middle of the pile.
3 *Operators.* Only one operator is explicitly mentioned in the problem statement — the 'move' operator. This operator allows the solver to move rings from one peg to another.
4 *Operator restrictions.* There are three restrictions placed on the use of the 'move' operator:
    (a) the solver is allowed to move only one ring at a time;
    (b) the solver is not allowed to place a larger ring on top of a smaller ring;
    (c) the solver is not allowed to place rings anywhere except on one of the three pegs.

SAQ 2
Fill in the initial states and goals for:
(a) Solving a crossword puzzle clue.   (b) Playing noughts and crosses.
    Initial state: Initial state:
    Goal state: Goal state:

An *ill-defined problem*, that is, an ill-structured problem, is one in which little or no information is provided on the initial state, the goal state, the operators, or some combination of these. An example of an ill-defined problem is how to pass an examination in psychology. If you try to analyse such a problem in terms of initial and goal states, operators and operator restrictions, you'll see that the task is only vaguely defined. The initial state includes a list of examination questions, information about the number of questions you are required to answer, and the total amount of time allowed for the examination. In broad terms the goal state is 'getting the grade you want'. If you want a grade A, your answers will have to be better than the answers you might give if you would be happy just to pass the examination. How would you know whether you've provided answers that will gain a pass, or an A? That is, how can you tell when the goal has been achieved?

The operators that can be brought to bear — none of which is made explicit in the examination paper — are things like retrieval of information from memory (what did the lecturer say?), making notes of information, organizing information, deleting unusable information, planning an answer, writing, editing, and so forth. Some operators that might normally be used, such as asking other students what they think, or looking in books and notes, are explicitly forbidden, and operators such as writing are restricted by time constraints, so decisions have to be made about how to divide time between organizing and writing answers to each question.

In short, in ill-defined problems the solver has to help to define the problem. This point draws our attention to the fact that degree of problem structure comes down to a question of a solver's own knowledge. For instance, consider your experience with the Towers of Hanoi problem. The particular problem you solved was the 'three ring' problem, and if you had never seen the problem before, then it had to be spelled out to you in detail. Suppose I now said, 'Can you do the Hanoi problem for me again? We'll use five rings this time. I want you to transfer them from Peg B to Peg C'. The problem will now seem pretty well-defined to you, even though a lot of information about the initial state, goal state, operators and restrictions on operators has not been provided.

This is because you are able to augment the problem *givens* (the information provided at the beginning of a problem is often referred to as the problem givens, or 'given' information) with knowledge retrieved from long-term memory. When a solver's knowledge is taken into account, the boundary between ill- and well-defined problems becomes somewhat blurred. In fact, problems should be treated as having more or less definition, or structure, than others, rather than as belonging in one category or the other. For example, Greeno (1976) has pointed out that there are many problems that are quite well-defined even though problem solvers treat them in such ways that they have 'indefinite' goals (which should lead to their being classified as ill-defined problems). Greeno draws his examples from problem solving in geometry, in which students are often set the goal of, say, proving two triangles congruent. There are a number of ways in which such a goal can be achieved, and the solver need not have a specific set of goal features in mind at the start of the problem in order to *recognize a solution* when one has been achieved. According to Greeno, that is all a person needs in order to solve such problems — the ability to recognize a solution when it arises. In solving such problems, solvers work forward, gathering information that will be useful in achieving the goal.

In terms of everyday problems, which will make it easier to understand Greeno's ideas, imagine setting out to do your shopping for the weekend. The goal is to get in enough food to feed the family for three days. This goal is pretty indefinite, in that you don't have any specific meals in mind. When you get to the butcher's shop, you consider the meats on display as you wait your turn to be served. There's liver — but the kids don't like it. Everybody likes steak, so that's a possibility — but not at those prices. What about that turkey? They all like turkey; you haven't prepared a turkey for a long time; you have all the other ingredients you need; the leftovers can be used to make a curry (another meal). This is a clear example of information gathering during the process of solving a problem, and fitting it in with the problem givens — family likes and dislikes, how much time you are prepared to spend on preparing meals, what other ingredients you already have that would make a particular meal possible, and so on. In other words, since at the beginning of the problem the goal was not completely pre-specified, this type of problem would have been considered as ill-defined. But we see that once a solver recognizes a situation as a satisfactory goal state (turkey dinner), the problem can be viewed as well-defined because the initial state of the problem (nothing for dinner), the operators (broadly speaking, all those actions involved in preparing a meal), and the operator restrictions (family likes and dislikes; possession of other necessary ingredients; price) are all there. The whole thing comes together as a well-defined problem when the information-gathering process delivers up a well-defined goal state.

Another everyday example would be 'getting away from it all'. You could pack the kids and your spouse/partner into the car and just head out into the country with the indefinite goal of 'having a good time'. You might see a place that would be nice for a picnic. (And, of course, you might *not* see a place that would be nice for a picnic, in which case the idea of having a picnic would perhaps not occur to you.) Or you might discover a village that would be nice for sightseeing. In short, possible solutions arise while you are working on the problem of having a nice day out, and, because you know the things you like doing, you are able to recognize situations that satisfy your goal. Greeno argues that the addition of problems with indefinite goals to the category of problems described as well-defined considerably broadens the boundaries of well-defined problems.

SAQ 3
Would you consider the problem of getting from London to Paris a well-defined problem or an ill-defined problem? Why?

Summary of Section 1

- A person has a 'problem' when he or she has a goal which cannot be achieved directly.
- Any action taken by a person in pursuit of a blocked goal, whether physical or mental, is regarded as problem solving.
- A major goal of problem-solving research is to devise a method which will make it possible to categorize the structures of problems and investigate successful problem-solving strategies.
- Some of the best researched problems in psychology belong to a class called transformation problems, which involve 'moves' that transform one state into another. The analysis of people's behaviour in solving such problems has laid the foundation for understanding problem solving in more complex situations.
- Researchers construct toy worlds like the Towers of Hanoi problem in which to study problem-solving processes because the short solution times and the fact that no prior knowledge is required allow them to study people's problem-solving strategies.
- One way of classifying problems is in terms of the degree to which they can be described as well-defined or ill-defined.
- Well-defined problems are those for which the initial state, goal state, and legal operators and operator restrictions are all given at the start of the problem.
- An ill-defined problem is one in which information about either the initial or goal state, or the operators and operator restrictions, is incomplete and has to be supplied by the problem solver.

2   *Analysing problem structures*

Two problems can seem quite different 'on the surface' but they may in fact have the same underlying problem structure — and as a result also have the same solution. Interestingly, when people are given problems having identical underlying structures but different 'cover stories', they often fail to detect the close relationship between the problems (concrete examples of this phenomenon will be demonstrated below). In this case, knowing the solution to one problem does not make the solution to the second problem easier. Moreover, even when people are told that such a relationship exists, they often fail to benefit from the solution of one of the problems in their attempt at solving the other. However, it is not sufficient merely to claim that problems that 'look different on the surface' are 'really the same underneath'. What is required is some rigorous method for revealing the underlying structure of problems. One such method is called *state space analysis* — and it has been used to investigate questions about how previous experience in solving a problem impacts on later attempts to solve related problems.

2.1   *State space analysis*

State space analysis is an important tool first of all in providing a representation of the underlying structure of problems. State space analysis involves constructing a diagram containing complete information about everything a solver could do, using only the rules of the problem. In order to demonstrate this notion, consider Figure 1.2 which shows the initial state (or state 1) of the Towers of Hanoi problem which you were asked to solve in Activity 1.

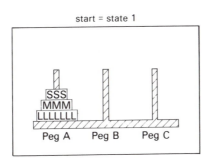

Figure 1.2

Given the rules of the game (only one ring can be moved at a time, and no ring can be placed on top of a smaller one), there are two possible 'legal' moves from state 1: move the small ring from Peg A to either Peg B or Peg C. Figure 1.3 shows the problem states that would result from making either of these two moves: that is, state 2 or state 3. The lines linking state 1 with state 2 and state 1 with state 3 stand for the application of the move operators (i.e. 'move the small ring from Peg A to Peg B' or 'move the small ring from Peg A to Peg C') which transform one state of the problem into another state.

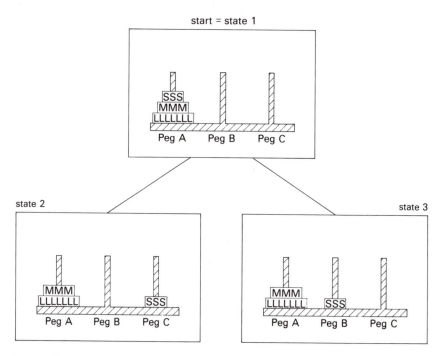

Figure 1.3

At state 2 of the problem, three moves are possible under the rules. First, the small ring could be moved back to its original position on Peg A, which is equivalent to undoing the original move (i.e. 'first move the small ring from Peg A to Peg C and then move it from Peg C back to Peg A'). This move would result in returning to state 1. Secondly, the small ring could be moved to Peg B, which would transform state 2 into state 3. Finally, the medium-sized ring could be moved from Peg A to Peg B, a move that would lead to a new state of the problem, state 4. In Figure 1.4, each of these moves is indicated by one of the lines emanating from state 2 of the problem. A line linking one state with another indicates the move possibilities between problem states. Thus, we could go from state 1 to state 2 (small ring from Peg A to Peg C) to state 4 (medium-sized ring from Peg A to Peg B), and back to

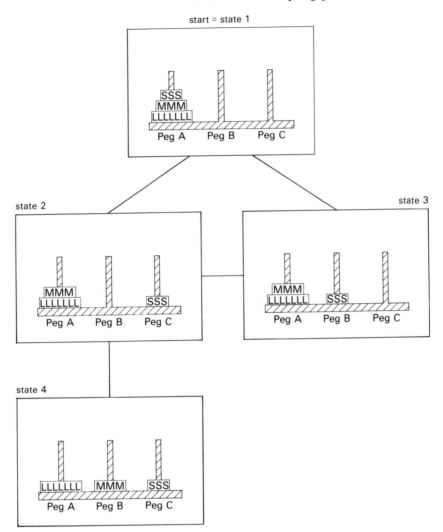

Figure 1.4

state 2 (medium-sized ring from Peg B to Peg A), and then on to state 3 (small ring from Peg C to Peg B) in the state space that has been developed so far. (If we made such a sequence of moves, we wouldn't be very good problem solvers, of course.)

SAQ 4
(a) Extend the state space on Figure 1.4 for the next possible move from state 3.
(b) List the states to which it is possible to go by moves from state 3. (There are altogether 27 states in the three-ring Towers of Hanoi problem. The entire state space will be given in the answer to this SAQ.)

25

Part I   Introduction to Problem Solving

2.2   *Isomorphic and homomorphic problems*

In this section we shall look at research on the way certain well-defined problems relate to one another. We shall begin with an activity.

Activity 2
Consider the following problem, called the *Chinese Tea Ceremony problem* (adapted from Hayes and Simon, 1974). Spend a few minutes trying to solve it.

A most civilized and refined tea ceremony is practised in the inns of certain Himalayan villages. The ceremony involves a host and exactly two guests, neither more nor less. One of the guests is more senior in rank to the other guest. When his guests have arrived and have seated themselves at his table, the host performs three services for them. These services are listed below in the order of nobility which the Himalayans attribute to them:

> Stoking the fire (least noble task)
> Pouring the tea (medium nobility)
> Reciting poetry (noblest task).

During the ceremony, any of those present may ask another person, 'Honoured Sir, may I perform this onerous task for you?' However, a person may ask to do only the least noble of the tasks which the other is currently performing. Further, if a person is currently performing any tasks, then he may not ask to do a task which is nobler than the least noble task he is already performing. Custom requires that, by the time the tea ceremony is over, all the tasks will have been transferred from the host to the more senior of the guests. How may this be accomplished?

SAQ 5
Fill in the details for the Chinese Tea Ceremony problem.
Initial state: Operators:
Goal state: Operator restrictions:

Did you recognize the similarities between the Chinese Tea Ceremony and the Towers of Hanoi problems? The 'three people' (Host, Junior Guest, and Senior Guest) in the Chinese Tea Ceremony problem are equivalent to the 'three pegs' in the Towers of Hanoi problem. The tasks are equivalent to rings. The degree of nobility of the different tasks is equivalent to the size of the three rings. The 'Ask' operator in the Chinese Tea Ceremony problem corresponds to the 'Move' operator in the Towers of Hanoi problem. In the Towers of Hanoi problem, no ring may be placed on top of a smaller one; in the Chinese Tea

Ceremony problem, no one can ask to perform a task 'nobler' than the least noble one the other is currently performing. In the Towers of Hanoi problem, the solver is explicitly told that only one ring may be moved at a time, but in the Chinese Tea Ceremony problem this particular operator restriction is implicit in the statement that 'a person may ask to do only the least noble of the tasks which the other is currently performing'.

How can we describe precisely the correspondences between the two different problems? This precision, as you may have suspected, can be achieved by drawing a complete diagram of move possibilities and states for both problems, and comparing the resulting state spaces. The Towers of Hanoi and Chinese Tea Ceremony problems are both known as transformation problems because the rules specify operators (moves) for transforming each state to another state in a state space.

In Figure 1.5 the initial state of the Chinese Tea Ceremony problem is presented along with the equivalent representation of the initial state of the Towers of Hanoi problem. In Figure 1.5 the Junior Guest is represented as 'Guest (J)' and the Senior Guest as 'Guest (S)'. Also, 'R' stands for the task of 'reciting poetry', 'P' stands for 'pouring tea', and 'S' stands for 'stoking the fire'.

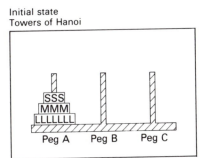

Figure 1.5

At the start of the Chinese Tea Ceremony problem, either of the guests can ask to perform the least noble task being performed by the Host, who is the only person performing tasks at the start of the problem. Figure 1.6 (overleaf) shows the results of performing the operations.

SAQ 6
What is the minimum number of moves needed to solve the Chinese Tea Ceremony problem? *Hint*: Look back to the answer to SAQ 1 (i.e. the Towers of Hanoi answer).

SAQ 7
The first few move possibilities in the Chinese Tea Ceremony problem are given in Figure 1.7 overleaf. Fill in the blank boxes in states 6, 7, 8 and 9 with the states that would result from legal moves from state 4 and state 5.

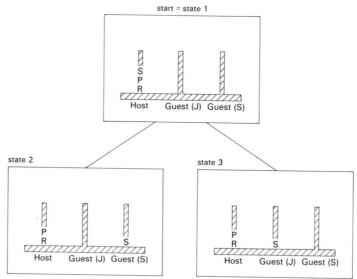

Figure 1.6

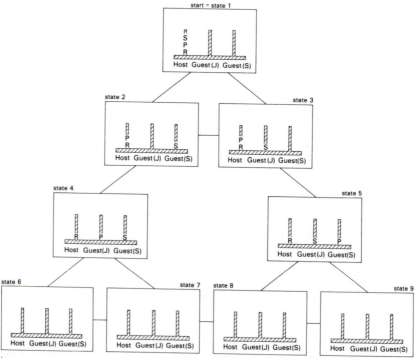

Figure 1.7

28

When we use the same notation to depict states in the two problems, we see that the two state spaces are *identical*. Only the physical details of the problems (tasks or rings, people or pegs, and so on) are different. When two problems can be represented by an identical state space, these two problems are said to be *isomorphic problems*. In general, an isomorph of something is anything with identical structure or form. Thus, state space representations allow us to compare different problems, to see if there is a correspondence in the underlying structure of the problem.

Now consider two other problems which are related to each other: the *Missionaries and Cannibals problem* and the *Jealous Husbands problem*.

The *Missionaries and Cannibals problem* is as follows:

Three missionaries and three cannibals seek to cross a river from the left bank to the right bank (as in Figure 1.8 below). They have a boat which can carry at most two people at a time. All missionaries and cannibals are able to navigate the boat. If at any time the cannibals outnumber the missionaries on either bank of the river, the missionaries will be eaten. Find the smallest number of crossings that will permit all the missionaries and cannibals to cross the river safety.

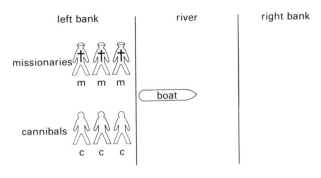

Figure 1.8

A state space diagram of the legal moves in the Missionaries and Cannibals problem is presented in Figure 1.9 overleaf. The problem can be solved in eleven moves, but people seldom get a solution in the minimum number of moves. This is because the problem contains a 'tricky state' (state 8, in Figure 1.9). It's 'tricky' because in order to progress towards the goal the solver has to move one Missionary and one Cannibal from the right side of the river *back* to the left side, which seems counterintuitive because the move results in *fewer* Missionaries and Cannibals on the goal side of the river at state 9. People are very reluctant to make this move. This situation (state 9) is in fact quite like a previous state of the problem, state 4, in which two Missionaries and two Cannibals were on the left side of the river and one Missionary and one Cannibal on the right side. The crucial difference between these two states is the position of the boat. The move from state 1 of the problem to state 4 puts the boat on the right-hand side of the river, while the move from state 8 to state 9 would leave the boat on the left-hand side of the river.

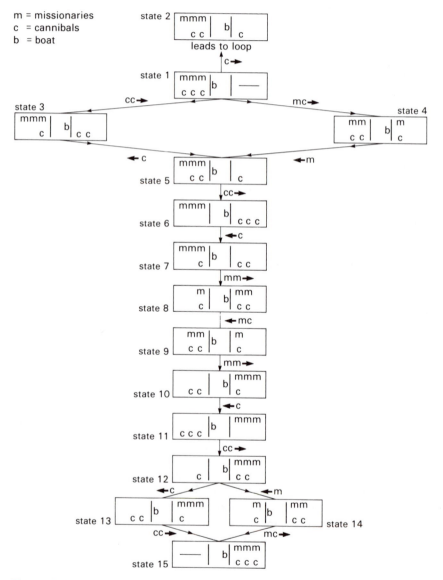

Figure 1.9

The *Jealous Husbands problem* involves moving three men and their wives: in this respect it is quite analogous to the Missionaries and Cannibals problem. But, in the form in which this problem was posed by Reed, Ernst and Banerji (1974), an additional constraint was imposed: because the husbands were jealous, a lone wife could not be left alone with a husband unless his own wife was present. In the Missionaries and Cannibals problem it doesn't make any difference which cannibals and missionaries are paired for a river crossing or which are left together on one bank or the other. Because of the restrictions concerning pairings of husbands and wives, the Jealous Husbands problem is harder than the Missionaries and Cannibals problem. Interestingly, both of these problems still have the same underlying structure when only legal moves are considered, but the Jealous Husbands problem has more illegal move possibilities than the Missionaries and Cannibals problem. Problems with a similar but not identical structure are called *homomorphic problems*.

Summary of Section 2

- A state space analysis of a problem provides us with a representation of the underlying structure of a problem.
- A state space diagram depicts all possible transformations between all legal states of a problem, connected by legal moves (operators).
- State space diagrams can be used as a tool for determining the relationship between the structures of two or more problems. It is important to emphasize that a state space diagram is a method used by researchers for analysing problems, not something that human problem solvers construct as they are solving problems.
- Problems which can be represented with identical state space diagrams are called isomorphic, or problem isomorphs. Problems with similar state space diagrams are called homomorphic, or problem homomorphs.

3 Analysis of problem solving

Up to now we have been concerned with specifying the *structures* of problems in terms of all possible moves. However, in this section and the next we shall be looking at the sequences of moves which problem solvers actually choose. Using state space analysis the problem-solving behaviour of subjects can be analysed by looking at the paths which they follow through the state space of a problem. Paths through problems of related structures can be compared to see to what extent the basic problem structure affects subjects' behaviour and to what extent differences emerge as a result of the different superficial details of the problem statement. The following Activity and SAQ illustrate the point about different paths that different people take through a state space when solving problems, and provide you with an opportunity to practise what you know about constructing state space diagrams.

Activity 3

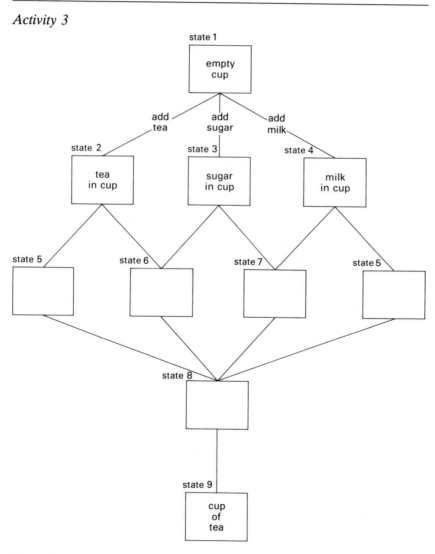

Figure 1.10

The following operators (moves) are involved in solving the everyday problem of making a cup of tea. Assume that you already have a cup, a pot of tea brewing, and so on:

ADD MILK TO CUP   = ADD MILK
STIR TEA   = STIR
ADD TEA TO CUP   = ADD TEA
ADD SUGAR TO CUP = ADD SUGAR

The state space diagram for this activity is presented in Figure 1.10. The initial state, the goal state and the states reachable from the initial state have already been filled in. The links between the initial state and its immediate successors have also been labelled with the operators that transform the initial state into the others. Fill in the rest of the diagram with appropriate operator labels on the links and the resultant states. The answer appears on page 56.

SAQ 8
Mark the boxes representing the moves you as an individual problem solver (tea maker) would take through the state space.

You might want to complain that making a cup of tea is not really a problem. If you already know how to solve a problem (that is, if you have learned a routine for dealing with certain situations, such as making tea), then your activity might not be described as problem solving. But making a cup of tea for the first time, for example, as a child, is certainly a problem. You might consider that a child has not learned how to make a cup of tea until the child takes the same path through the state space as you take (for example, pouring the milk into the cup before adding hot tea, or whatever). And even then, if you consider the finer details of the performance, you will probably agree that there is more to making a cup of tea (or playing tennis, or solving any other problem) than just knowing the routine. In fact, my sons often complain that I don't know how to make a 'proper' cup of tea, even though I follow the same steps: stick a tea bag in a cup, pour boiling water on it, stare at it for a bit, remove the tea bag, add some milk and stir. My eldest son complains that I leave the tea bag in for too long (or not long enough — there's no pleasing him). According to my critics, I need to 'tune' my 'stare at it for a bit' operator. But since I don't drink tea myself, I may never get it right. The example draws our attention to the point that some tasks or problems can be done better or worse (for example, playing tennis, making tea) and the quality does not depend on the order or identity of the moves made but on fine details of the way in which each separate move is performed.

3.1   *Problem representations*

People differ in the way they solve problems for a number of reasons. One of the most important determinants of the ease with which a problem can be solved, or even whether it can be solved at all, is the way the solver constructs a mental representation of the problem. In other words, different people have different ways of seeing situations (including formal problems presented in psychological laboratories), and the way they see a situation largely determines what they'll do in that situation. As a mundane example, consider a situation in which a man and a woman are seen in heated argument in a public place. Let's say that one of the two (it makes no difference which it is for the purpose of the point I want to make) is gesticulating more, making more noise, seems to be dominating the action. Now imagine a couple of extreme stereotypical onlookers — a male chauvinist and a fanatical women's libber. You undoubtedly can imagine (given that we are here talking about extreme stereotypes) what either of these two might think about the activity they are observing.

Another example comes from Hayes (1978), who uses the following pair of examples to illustrate the issue of problem representation.

Activity 4

Consider an ordinary 64-square checkerboard in which the squares in two diagonally opposite corners have been removed, as in Figure 1.11. If you had 31 dominoes, each of which would cover exactly two squares on the checkerboard, is there any way you could arrange the dominoes so that all the remaining 62 squares would be covered? If you think you could, how would you prove it? And if you think not, how would you prove that?

Most people find this a hard problem, especially the proof. The problem is easier to solve (and prove) if it is presented in more everyday terms.

Activity 5

Imagine that you are a matchmaker, and that you have been summoned to some remote village which contains exactly 64 unmarried young people, 32 men and 32 women. Your job is to pair up the couples in time for a group wedding two days hence, a Saturday morning. You work throughout the day and all day Friday, before you eventually succeed in matching couples to the satisfaction of everybody concerned. But, that evening, during pre-wedding celebrations, two of the men get into a fight and kill one another. Can all the 62 remaining young people get married on Saturday morning as planned.

Figure 1.11

You can use your solution to the matchmaker problem as a basis for solving the problem about the mutilated checkerboard, if you haven't solved it already. The checkerboard contains squares of alternating colours. Every white square (i.e. 'woman' in the matchmaker problem) is bordered by a black square (i.e. 'man' in the matchmaker problem). A domino placed on two squares (i.e. a successful matchmaking in the matchmaker problem) must by necessity cover a black square and a white square. But in the mutilated checkerboard two black squares (two men) are missing. Hence, the 62 remaining squares cannot be covered by 31 dominoes. Simon (1978) points out that people do not

Part I   Introduction to Problem Solving

always construct an optimal representation of a problem. But the way a problem is presented can help them to achieve a more useful representation.

The important issue of *problem representation* was investigated by Simon and Hayes (1976), who examined the consequences of different verbal formulations of a given problem in order to gain some insight into how problem statements are initially understood by problem solvers. Simon and Hayes used several isomorphic variations on the Towers of Hanoi problem. In some variations the rules of the problem specified legal moves in terms of size changes (for example, magically shrinking globes). Other variations stuck to the idea of physically moving items from one place to another. To give you some idea of the difficulties people experience in understanding problems with a different cover story but the same underlying structure, here is the statement of (a) a *move problem,* and (b) a *change problem,* both of which were used in studies by Simon and Hayes. As you read the problems, you should try to note what difficulties you yourself have in understanding them.

(a)   a move problem
Three five-handed extraterrestrial monsters were holding three crystal globes. Because of the quantum-mechanical peculiarities of their neighbourhood, both monsters and globes came in exactly three sizes — small, medium and large — and no other sizes were permitted. The medium-sized monster was holding the small globe; the small monster was holding the large globe; and the large monster was holding the medium-sized globe. Since this situation offended their keenly developed sense of symmetry, they proceeded to transfer globes from one to another so that each monster would have a globe proportionate to its own size. Monster etiquette complicated the solution to the problem because it required that:
1 only one globe could be moved at a time;
2 if a monster was holding two globes, only the larger of the two could be moved;
3 a globe could not be moved to a monster who was holding a larger globe.
By what sequence of transformations could the monsters have solved this problem?

(b)   a change problem
Three five-handed extraterrestrial monsters were holding three crystal globes. Because of the quantum-mechanical peculiarities of their neighbourhood, both monsters and globes came in exactly three sizes — small, medium and large — and no other sizes were permitted. The medium-sized monster was holding the small globe; the small monster was holding the large globe; and the large monster was holding the

medium-sized globe. Since this situation offended their keenly developed sense of symmetry, they proceeded to shrink and expand the globes so that each monster would have a globe proportionate to its own size. Monster etiquette complicated the solution to the problem because it required that:

1 only one globe could be shrunk or expanded at a time;
2 if two globes were of the same size, only the globe held by the larger monster could be shrunk or expanded;
3 a globe could not be shrunk or expanded to the same size as the globe of a larger monster.

By what sequence of changes could the monsters have solved this problem?

Simon and Hayes presented different groups of subjects with either a move problem or a change problem. Their results showed that move problems were solved in about half the time needed to solve the change problems. The problem variations had a strong influence on the representations adopted by the subjects when they attempted to solve the problems (as revealed by the comments they made during their problem solving). Kotovsky, Hayes and Simon (1985) have concluded that the problem structure alone, as reflected in the state space analysis, is not enough to predict the kind of difficulties a subject might have in solving a problem. The task of 'understanding' the problem itself, that is, of adopting some internal representation of the states and operators, has a drastic effect on problem solving, because some representations might involve much simpler processing operations than others.

Summary of Section 3

- Problem-solving strategies can be analysed in terms of the paths of moves taken by an individual solver through a state space.
- Structural factors, such as problems having an identical and clear state space structure, and psychological factors, such as instructions and the number of mental steps involved in solving the problem, both have an effect on problem-solving strategies.
- The way a person represents a problem strongly influences the ease with which the problem can be solved, or whether it can be solved.

4   Transfer of problem-solving skills

One of the dominating questions in problem-solving research concerns the effects of experience on subsequent problem-solving efforts. The first time we are confronted with a particular problem, we may experience difficulties in solving it. But when we are faced with the same problem again and again, or with a series of similar problems, we expect to get better and better as we benefit from our experience. Improved performance as a result of solving a number of similar problems is a phenomenon called *positive transfer*. Sometimes, though, the effects of experience can result in *negative transfer*. This occurs when previous experience interferes with the solution to a current problem.

For example, if England changed the colour of green traffic lights to blue, we could expect people to learn to 'go' at blue lights fairly quickly (positive transfer of our knowledge of green lights). But imagine the consequences of reversing the colours: red to go, and green to stop. Your old knowledge would definitely (and perhaps fatally) interfere (negative transfer).

Transfer effects have been studied by presenting a subject with problems which may appear different in their surface characteristics but which have the same or a very similar underlying structure.

4.1   Transfer effects between well-defined problems

A number of interesting questions have been asked about the behaviour of people solving transformation problems, and in particular their behaviour on problems that can be shown to have the same, or similar, underlying structure, but perhaps different cover stories. In this section we shall explore two questions that are of enduring importance:

1 Does experience on a given problem make it easier for subjects to solve new problems which are isomorphic (or nearly so) to the original problem (positive transfer)?
2 How do different kinds of cover stories affect the solution time and moves subjects choose to make through a state space?

In an attempt to provide an answer to the first question, Reed, Ernst and Banerji (1974) sought to discover whether skill acquired in performing one task could be transferred to homomorphic problems. The tasks they used were the Missionaries and Cannibals problem and the Jealous Husbands problem, both of which have already been discussed in Section 2.1. The results are described in Techniques Box A.

TECHNIQUES BOX A

Reed, Ernst and Banerji (1974)

Rationale
Reed, Ernst and Banerji predicted that subjects who are given problems with similar problem states would show improved performance on the second problem.

Method
Subjects were asked to solve two problems — Missionaries and Cannibals and then Missionaries and Cannibals again; or Jealous Husbands and then Jealous Husbands again; or Missionaries and Cannibals and then Jealous Husbands; or Jealous Husbands and then Missionaries and Cannibals. In addition, some subjects in the last two conditions were explicitly told about the relationship between the two problems. Data was collected on the total number of moves involved in solving each problem, and the number of illegal moves attempted.

Results
When subjects were presented with identical problems (Missionaries and Cannibals then Missionaries and Cannibals, or Jealous Husbands then Jealous Husbands), there was improved performance, in that fewer moves were required to solve the problem the second time (see Table 1.1). Subjects who were given the Jealous Husbands problem followed by the Missionaries and Cannibals problem improved their performance on the second problem only when the relationship between the two problems was revealed by the experimenter. Subjects who received the Missionaries and Cannibals problem followed by the Jealous Husbands problem showed no improvement, even when the relationship was revealed by the experimenter.

Table 1.1

Problem 1	Problem 2	Improvement
M and C	M and C	YES
JH	JH	YES
M and C	JH	NO (no hint)
JH	M and C	NO (no hint)
M and C	JH	NO (hint)
JH	M and C	YES (hint)

The results from the Reed *et al.* experiment show: (1) that experience with a particular problem facilitates further attempts at solving the same problem again; and (2) that experience with an earlier problem only facilitates solution of a second related problem if (a) the second problem is simpler than the first, and (b) a hint is given that the two problems are related. Hence the subjects' failure to improve their performance on the Jealous Husbands problem after experience solving the Missionaries and Cannibals problem, even when the relationship between the problems was pointed out. These are surprising results, in that they suggest that if people are left to themselves they are not very good at bringing their previous experience to bear in solving related problems.

In another experiment, Luger and Bauer (1978) sought to discover whether skill acquired performing one task could be transferred to a second, identical (isomorphic) task, if the tasks have a clear sub-problem structure.

The Towers of Hanoi problem has a pretty obvious sub-goal structure to it, as shown in its state space analysis, and most people, with a little experience on the problem, can work out what that structure is. The Towers of Hanoi problem can be broken down into sub-problems. For example, to solve the three-ring Towers of Hanoi problem it is necessary at some point to move the largest of the three rings from its original position on Peg A to Peg B. But before this can be done the two smaller rings must be assembled in their proper order on Peg C. The problem of moving two rings from one peg to another may be called a two-ring sub-problem, and constitutes a natural sub-part of the state space of the three-ring problem. Some people understand a lot about the Towers of Hanoi problem simply from reading its description. For instance, they don't usually move the same ring twice in succession — they don't take the small ring off Peg A and place it on Peg B, then take if off Peg B and place it on Peg C, because they understand just enough of the problem to see that this is a waste of time when the same effect could be achieved by simply taking the ring off Peg A and placing it directly on Peg C. They also rarely undo the last move they have made: for example, by taking the small ring off Peg A and placing it on Peg B and then taking it off Peg B and placing it right back on Peg A. Moves that subjects normally avoid reflect something of their limited understanding of the Towers of Hanoi problem when it is first presented to them. Other transformation tasks, such as the Missionaries and Cannibals problem, do not have such an obvious problem structure.

In their experiment Luger and Bauer presented one group of subjects with the Towers of Hanoi problem followed by the Chinese Tea Ceremony problem, and another group with the Chinese Tea Ceremony problem followed by the Towers of Hanoi problem. Neither group of subjects was told that the two problems were related. Luger and Bauer argued that the isomorphic relationship between the two problems would lead to a transfer of learning, reflected in improved performance on the second task. They measured the total time both groups took to solve both problems as well as the number of states entered and the number of illegal moves attempted. The results confirmed their prediction about transfer of learning between the tasks in both conditions. These results show that identical problems with a clear sub-problem structure can enhance transfer of learning from one task to another. Luger and Bauer suggested that the lack of clear sub-problem structure in the Missionaries and Cannibals problem could account for the lack of transfer on the problems in the Reed *et al.* study. Taken together, these results also indicate that problem structure is important in determining problem difficulty.

Summary of Section 4

- Transfer of learning research involves understanding how material learned at one point in time affects the learning of other material. Experience with earlier tasks may either faciliate (positive transfer) or hinder (negative transfer) the solving of related material.
- Experimental studies on transformation problems such as Missionaries and Cannibals and Jealous Husbands show that experience on a problem does not necessarily transfer to another problem of the same type unless people are aware of the similarity and the second problem is simpler than the first.
- Transfer is facilitated if different problems have a related, sub-goal structure.

5   Information-processing models of the problem solver

The next few pages are devoted to an overview of the information-processing theory of human problem solving put forward by Simon (1978). Simon's theory characterizes problem solving as an interaction between a *task environment* (that is, a problem) and a problem solver, who is thought of as an information-processing system. According to Simon, the problem structure itself constrains the processes of problem solving, in that it contains considerable information about what the problem is and what needs to be done in order to solve it. As we have seen in previous sections, problems often contain information about the initial state of the problem, the goal, and the operators that can be used to achieve the goal. Problem information also often rules out certain actions: for example, in the Towers of Hanoi problem the operator restrictions rule out the possibility of simply moving the whole tower of rings over in one move. This is not to claim that people always understand perfectly the tasks with which they find themselves confronted, or that they will invariably be able to solve problems even given that they have a perfect understanding of what the problem is. The claim is simply that people approach problems rationally (to the extent that they are capable of rationality) and that problems themselves contain a lot of information that can be used to guide solution processes.

5.1 Knowledge states

In order to solve problems people must construct a *mental representation* of the given problem information, as we have already seen in Section 1.2: initial state, goal state, operators, and operator restrictions. Simon refers to this mental representation of the problem as the person's *problem space*. What we have referred to as a state space diagram represents an omniscient observer's view of the structure of a problem. It is important to keep this distinction in mind: the problem space is a person's individual representation of a problem, and as such may contain more or less information than that given in the problem statement. For example, when you read the Towers of Hanoi problem description you presumably inferred that you could look at the coins as you moved them from one circle to another, although the description of the problem contained no information either permitting or forbidding 'watching what you are doing'. In fact, many problem descriptions contain such implicit information. Thus, an essential idea behind the notion of a person's individual problem space as discussed by Simon is that when confronted with a problem people bring to bear that part of their total store of knowledge that is (or that they think is) relevant to the problem at hand. People try to relate what they understand about a particular problem to specific knowledge they have about problems of that type.

During the course of solving a problem, a solver progresses through a sequence of *knowledge states*. A knowledge state contains the information a person has available at each point in the problem-solving process, or which can be made available (for example, by retrieving knowledge from long-term memory). Transformation of a knowledge state is accomplished by applying *mental operations* to change it into another knowledge state. You have probably noticed that the terminology used by Simon is very similar to the way we described state space analysis of problems in terms of states and operations for moving from one state to the next. The crucial difference is that we are now talking not about the objective structure of a problem but about the *mental* knowledge states and *mental* operations going on inside the problem solver's head. This has the important effect of allowing for individual differences between problem solvers.

5.2   The role of memory

Simon also stresses that problem solving is greatly influenced by properties of the information-processing system, such as the capacity of working memory and the amount of time involved in storage and retrieval processes in long-term memory. If working memory is only capable of holding a few units of information, and optimal performance on a task requires that more states and rules need to be considered, then performance will be less than optimal. Consider the working memory load involved in having to remember a telephone number just long enough to dial it. Read the number at the end of this sentence (once only) and then try to repeat it back immediately: 9376054. Now let's make the problem a bit harder. Imagine that you find a message asking you to call someone from a particular company at a particular number. Read the information that follows this sentence (again, once only) and then try to repeat it, in the same order. Mr Kresge, General Insurance Company, 2585492.

It has been estimated by Simon that working memory (WM) is limited to about five *chunks*, where a chunk 'corresponds to anything that has become a meaningful unit of experience' (Simon, 1974): for example, your own telephone number, a concept such as 'criminal lawyer', or even an adage such as 'Women and children first'. The important point here is that the size of a chunk is variable. Learning a new telephone number involves holding about seven of ten familiar chunks of information (the numerals from 0 to 9) just long enough to dial them. A different example would be learning a list of items to be purchased on a trip to the supermarket. A final example would be learning an ordered list of aphorisms with which you are already familiar, such as 'Spare the rod and spoil the child', 'Too many cooks spoils the broth', 'He who lingers is lost', and so on. It is generally regarded that the number of chunks that can be held in working memory at any one time is seven, plus or minus two (Miller, 1956), although Simon (1974) has argued that the number is closer to five.

Although working memory capacity limits performance, the limitation is considered to present only very general constraints on problem-solving performance in everyday life because a solver may extend the capacity of short-term memory by writing and referring to notes or intermediate results during the course of problem solving.

Another way to reduce the load on WM is to have crucial information stored in long-term memory (LTM). All the facts a person knows, and procedures for solving problems, are stored in LTM, and such knowledge has an effect on the way problems are solved since an individual obviously draws on previous experience (e.g. the rules of arithmetic, how to mix paints, where books and writing materials are kept, etc.) when confronted by a new problem. Also important are interactions between working memory and long-term memory. Kotovsky *et al.* (1985) have shown that people are unable to plan a sequence of moves on complex puzzle-like problems until they have spent a considerable amount of time in learning problem rules and practising rule application. For example, consider again the following rules from a variant of the move and change problems discussed in Section 3.1 (isomorphs of the Towers of Hanoi (TOH) problem), but with monsters and globes changed to boxes and dots.

Activity 6

This activity is in two parts (and if you do it properly, you may find it will take up some considerable time; it's worth the time to teach yourself something about the role of memory in problem solving).

Part 1

Get somebody to test you while you read the following rule, called a *move* rule. Take as much time reading it as you think you need in order to repeat the rule back out loud. The other person should time you from the moment you indicate you are ready to start reading until you look up and say you are ready to repeat the rule from memory. If you can't repeat the rule back twice without making a mistake, go back to reading again until you think you've got it right. Keep track of the number of times you have to go back to reading the rule (and the total amount of time) before you can repeat it out loud twice. Don't go on to the second part of the activity until you've successfully completed this first part.

> *Move rule:*   If two dots are touching the same box, only the larger dot may be moved.

Part 2

Now, look at Figure 1.12, which contains (a) an intermediate state in a move problem (labelled the 'current state' in the figure, and (b) a 'next state'). Without looking back to the formal statement of the rule, you should say as quickly as possible whether or not the 'next state' represents a legal move from the 'current state', given the rule you've memorized.

In this case, the transformation represents a legal move, since the larger of the two dots touching the left-most box has been moved to the middle box.

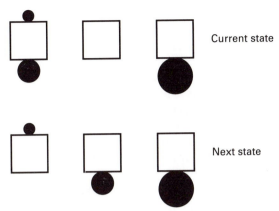

Figure 1.12

Now here's another Activity.

Activity 7

Part 1
This Activity is exactly like the previous one, except now you have to learn a *change* rule. Use the same procedure as in the previous Activity.

    Change rule: A dot may not be changed to the same size as a dot touching a smaller box.

Part 2
Is the 'next state' in Figure 1.13 a legal state from the 'current state' in the figure, given the 'change' rule you've just memorized?

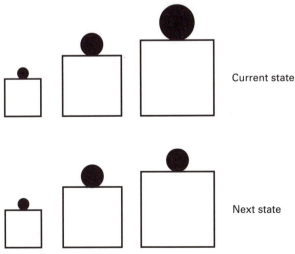

Figure 1.13

In this case, the transformation represents an illegal move because the large globe on the largest box has been changed to the same size as the globe on a smaller box — the one in the middle.

Kotovsky *et al.* performed an intriguing series of experiments in order to determine what made some versions of this problem (i.e. the TOH problem) harder than others. They found that some rules are *a lot harder to learn* than others (I suspect you found the change rule considerably harder to learn than the move rule in the two previous Activities), and that some rules were *much more difficult to apply* than others. One of their most interesting findings was that until subjects had considerable experience solving such problems they were unable to plan more than one step ahead. However, after a lot of experience, subjects suddenly found themselves able to plan about three moves ahead, particularly near the end of the problem. Kotovsky *et al.* attributed this improvement entirely to memory processes. Early in problem solving, subjects use up most of WM rehearsing the rules and trying to apply them; the more difficult the rule, the more WM is occupied with rehearsal and application. With practice, though, people 'overlearn' the rules and automate the rule-application process (that is, the rules are stored in LTM and are made readily accessible when required). Thus, some of the burden on WM is shifted to LTM. The extra WM capacity made available by this shift of information to LTM can then be employed in other aspects of processing, such as planning. Other research (e.g. Atwood and Polson, 1976) supports the view that LTM has an important role to play in reducing the load on WM during learning.

5.3   Development of heuristic strategies

Given that problem solving is characterized as mental transformations of problem states, a solver is always in the position of having to choose an operator for transforming a current knowledge state. One way to proceed from any knowledge state would simply be to apply all possible legal operators in order to generate all possible successor states, and to choose one of the successors as a new starting point for making further progress in the problem. Unfortunately, most problem spaces are quite large — even the simple three-ring Towers of Hanoi problem has a total of 27 different states — and human working memory capacity, as we have seen, is severely limited. In order to get around these limitations, people employ various *strategies* for guiding a search for solutions to problems.

The selection and evaluation of mental operators are characterized in Simon's theory as *heuristic search processes. Heuristics* are rule-of-thumb, problem-solving methods which often succeed but which do not guarantee a solution to a problem. A mundane example of a heuristic is, 'Ask for directions when lost in an unfamiliar place'. Asking local people how to get from one place to another and following their directions often does the trick; but you could follow a guide's instructions perfectly and still end up on the wrong side of a city if your guide was mistaken about the location of the place you wanted to get to or set out to mislead you. Heuristics are usually contrasted with *algorithms* or procedures which guarantee success if followed faithfully. The rules of arithmetic are good examples of algorithms.

5.4   *Means-ends analysis*

Many problems with a clearly defined goal state, which of course include transformation problems, can be solved using a general problem-solving strategy called *means-ends analysis*. The method was developed by Newell, Shaw and Simon (1958) in the *General Problem Solving* computer program (called *GPS*). Although many versions of GPS were designed only with the goal of making machines perform 'intelligently', some versions were designed with human performance limitations in mind. In a comparison of GPS with human problem solving on transformation problems, Newell and Simon (1972) concluded that much of human problem-solving behaviour could be characterized in terms of means-ends analysis.

Means-ends analysis works by determining *differences* between a current state of a problem and a goal state — differences between what you have now and what you want to end up with — and selecting operators known to be useful in reducing such differences. The basic idea behind means-ends analysis is that people have knowledge about the *means* (operators) at their disposal for achieving certain *ends*, or goals. Think of the various means you know about for achieving a goal such as 'getting down to the shops'. You could walk, drive your car, ride a bicycle, run, roller-skate, or take a bus. To see how means-ends analysis can help to build up a plan, consider the following (invented) protocol of me building a plan. My goal or *end* is to transform 'me at home' into 'me in Trafalgar Square'. The first task is to compare these two states and find the difference between them. I find the difference to be one of 'location'. The *means* I have of reducing differences of location are *operators*, such as 'walk' or 'go by train'. Some operators (for example, 'walk') can be rejected as not feasible, because I live fifty miles away in Milton Keynes and I am extremely lazy; but 'go by train' is feasible, so my next goal is to apply this operator to the initial state, 'me at home'. Unfortunately, the operator will not apply immediately because the conditions are not right — trains don't stop at my house. If I want to take a train I have to get to Milton Keynes Central Station. So I set up a new *sub-goal* to reduce the difference between 'me at home' and 'me at Milton Keynes Central Station'. Again, the difference is one of location and so again I refer to 'travel' operators. I can reject 'walk' as not feasible (I am lazy) and 'go by train' as a potential loop (I am already considering going by train from my home) and select 'go by taxi'. This cannot be applied because the conditions are wrong — the taxi driver doesn't know of my need for a taxi. The difference is one of information, so I look for an operator which can reduce differences of information, and find communication operators, such as 'use the telephone' ...

Means-ends analysis works, then, by analysing problems into goals and sub-goals by working out which moves (means) will attain the end-goal (means-ends analysis). Operators are selected that are known to be useful for achieving particular goals and sub-goals. This kind of analysis can be carried on to any required depth and will eventually produce a plan consisting of a sequence of *operators* which can be applied directly: walk into the kitchen, telephone for a taxi, be carried in the taxi to the train station, walk from the taxi into the station, and so on and so forth, until I find myself in Trafalgar Square.

Means-ends analysis is a very general problem-solving method, useful in a large number of problem-solving situations, including real-world situations involving considerable amounts of knowledge, such as the example just given. In order to plan a trip from, say, London to Pittsburgh, a solver needs to know a great deal about travel agencies, airports, money, and numerous other things. However, means-ends analysis may not always be the best way of solving any particular problem. In certain circumstances, it can even lead away from a solution to a problem. A mundane example is that of a bee repeatedly bouncing its nose against a window, trying to get out of a house (the most direct route to where it wants to be from where it is is straight ahead), rather than moving two feet to the left in order to exit through an open window.

Summary of Section 5

- Information-processing psychologists such as Simon view problem solving as search through a mental problem space.
- Both working memory and long-term memory have an important role to play in problem solving and learning. In the early stages of learning, a considerable burden is placed on working memory as new facts and operators are being acquired. With experience, some of this burden is shifted to long-term memory. When this happens, solvers begin to be able to plan sequences of moves in problem solving.
- Problem solvers bring their own knowledge to bear in constructing problem spaces and in searching for solutions to problems.

Heuristics are (imperfect) rules of thumb that guide search for a solution to a problem.

- Means-ends analysis is a powerful heuristic which involves breaking a problem down into goals and sub-goals until a point is reached at which specific actions can be taken to solve a problem.

6   Methods for studying problem solving

Just as in other areas of cognitive research, students of human problem solving need methods for investigating what goes on inside people's heads when they solve problems — you can't just look inside their heads and see what's going on in there. In this section we shall discuss three methods which have been used extensively by researchers trying to understand problem solving: *experiments*, *computer modelling*, and the analysis of *verbal protocols*.

6.1   Experiments

Researchers interested in problem solving typically use experimental methods to answer questions of interest to them. Experimental research takes many forms. In every case, the experimenter has an idea that some manipulation will have some effect on behaviour in a particular, controlled situation. It is interesting to consider where these ideas (hypotheses) come from. Ideally, they are derived from a theory of problem solving which is general enough to account for a wide range of experimental results that have already been collected, and from which further predictions about behaviour can be generated. But this is the ideal. Research can also be exploratory in nature (Kintsch, Miller and Polson, 1984). This kind of research often occurs when no overarching theory yet exists, often when there is an awakening of interest in a new research area or a re-awakening of interest in old problems that had been abandoned for one reason or another. In this situation, research is often necessarily exploratory rather than theory driven.

A good example of exploratory research has already been described in Section 4.1 above, where we described experiments by Reed, Ernst and Banerji which explored transfer effects between the Missionaries and Cannibals problem and the Jealous Husbands problem.

The main point about the experimental method is that it allows precise *measurement* of performance and *comparison* of performance under different conditions. As we have already seen, much can be inferred about the mental processes involved in solving a problem by comparison of measured performance under varying conditions.

6.2   Computer simulation models

Information-processing psychologists have been strongly influenced by research in *artificial intelligence (AI)*. AI researchers design computer programs that perform activities such as 'seeing', language understanding, or problem solving. AI researchers are interested in getting their programs to work, and to work efficiently, without being concerned with the way humans perform such tasks (although they are willing to use any available knowledge about human performance).

We need to draw a distinction between AI and *computer simulation* models of human behaviour. As already stated, AI researchers are interested in getting their programs to work, and to work efficiently, without being concerned with the way humans perform such tasks. In computer simulation, however, the goal is to design programs that match human performance closely, including errors. Information-processing psychologists such as Simon argue that a supreme test of a theory of cognitive behaviour is to specify the theory in such detail that it can be implemented as a computer simulation program which actually performs the behaviour the theory is trying to account for. To quote Polson and Jeffries (1982):

> Unlike a theory presented as descriptive prose, a process model of a task requires the concrete specification of the actions and decisions that a solver performs. Consider, for example, the selection of potential moves. A less specific theory might merely state that a move is selected for consideration, whereas the computer formalism forces us to decide the order in which moves are chosen. We can do this at different levels of detail, however. We can specify an order, which becomes a testable tenet of the theory.

Constructing a program that solves problems, even one that seems to display the same characteristics in solving problems as human solvers, demonstrates only one way in which the problem *could* be solved (we shall be returning to this point in particular, and other points raised here, in Section 5 of Part II where a computer model of human learning is described in some detail). A running program does not constitute proof that the mechanisms embodied in the program are the same mechanisms that underlie human performance. Other programs, with different mechanisms, might also mimic human performance. In such cases, various criteria must be used to decide between the models as embodied in computer programs.

A major advantage of a computer simulation of human problem solving is that it forces a theorist to be completely explicit about the information a problem solver uses and how that information is organized in memory. It also forces the theorist to be precise in specifying the processes that operate on stored information, and the control structure of the processing system — how processes are selected from one moment to the next.

6.3 Protocol analysis

Programs that embody models of human performance are often tested by comparing the step-by-step performance of the program with the step-by-step performance of a human solver. In order to obtain information about people's individual problem-solving strategies, unique methods are needed to gather data that allow us to make inferences about what is going on inside people's heads while they are working on a problem.

Data on human performance may be gathered by collecting a verbal account from the person solving the problem, known as a *verbal protocol*. Verbal protocols result from asking subjects to 'think aloud' while solving a problem, just as you were asked to do when attempting the problem presented in Activity 1. These verbalizations, plus whatever actions a person takes in solving a problem, are recorded and analysed phrase by phrase. Each phrase represents an assertion about the task or a single act of task-specific behaviour.

In order to illustrate *protocol analysis*, consider the fragment of a protocol presented in Table 1.2 overleaf. A first pass analysis of the first half of the protocol has been provided, to give you an idea of how such an analysis proceeds. The numbered lines contain the statements made by the subject, and the comments in brackets indicate the kind of mental processes that seem to be reflected in the preceding statements. This protocol is slightly bogus because:
1 It was taken by the same person who was doing the problem.
2 He was writing down the protocol instead of taping and transcribing it.
The goal of the first pass analysis is to identify the processes that occur. On a second pass the analyst might search for patterns among the processes identified on the first pass.

If you made a record of your thoughts in solving the Activity 1 problem, then you know what it is like to try to provide a researcher with a verbal protocol. In fact, obtaining a good verbal protocol from a subject is a difficult task. For one thing, subjects may report something different from what they actually did in an attempt to justify

Table 1.2

The problem
On Monday morning I had $132.48 in my account. During the week I made the following transactions: Cheque $12.25; Deposit 31.80; Cheque 20.15; Cheque 15.83. What's my balance now?

---

  1 So let's isolate the cheques to see how much I lost.
     (apply 'divide into like parts'-heuristic: cheques and deposit)
  2 Twenty-five and fifteen is forty ...
     (divide into cents part and dollars part sub-problems)
     (automatic, double column, well rehearsed (fives) addition process)
  3 plus eight-three ...
     (set up sub-problem for harder addition)
  4 is three [3] ...
     (fast zero addition)
  5 four and eight is twelve ...
     (addition fact recall)
  6 so that's one twenty-three [1.23] ...
     (finish sub-problem) (begin sub-problem for dollars part)
  7 twelve, twenty and fifteen is, let's see, thirty-five ...
     (fast addition 20 + 15 = 35)
  8 plus ... forty-seven ...
     (fast addition 35 + 12 = 47) (finish sub-problem)
  9 plus one twenty-three is forty-seven twenty-three
     (combine ... but forgot to add on 1.00!)
 10 Now that minus thirty-one eighty is how much I subtract ...
     (do the other half of the top goal division)
 11 so forty-seven twenty-three, less thirty-one eighty ...
     (sets up subtraction problem: 47.23 − 31.80 = ??)
 12 three ... zero ... three
 13 two ... eight
 14 carry ... no borrow ... twelve ... twelve
 15 eight ... four
 16 seven ...
 17 no six
 18 ... less one ... five
 19 four ... three
 20 Do I have to borrow again? ... No
 21 Four ... three ... one
 22 OK so one thirty-two forty-eight less fifteen forty-three is ...
 23 five cents
 24 Thirty minus fifteen plus two is fifteen ...
 25 seventeen, so ...
 26 it's one seventeen and five cents.

---

themselves. Many subjects find it difficult to talk about their spontaneous thought processes in the presence of another person or a tape recorder. In this situation, many of the thoughts are simply unavailable for study because they remain unspoken.

More worrying are the arguments of Nisbett and Wilson (1977), who claim that protocols are spurious evidence for cognitive processes because subjects do not have introspective access to the higher mental processes involved in problem solving. They argue that protocols are after-the-event rationalizations in which subjects offer hypotheses to explain what they are doing. However, because they have no access to their own thought processes, the subjects' reports are no more valid than the speculations of an external observer. In support of their view, Nisbett and Wilson cite numerous instances of introspections concerned with perception, emotion and problem solving where subjects are either unable to verbalize their reasoning, or are clearly inaccurate in doing so.

In defending the use of verbal protocols Ericsson and Simon (1980) have outlined two crucial issues:

1 Do verbal protocols accurately reflect underlying cognitive processes?
2 Does the production of a verbal protocol significantly distort the normal processes?

Ericsson and Simon argue that a protocol can be validated if there is a close correspondence between the statements in the protocol and the subject's behaviour. We constantly use this method in everyday situations. If someone said to you 'Wow, I'm hungry as a horse', then you expect that person to perform some action that will lead him to a meal. In the laboratory, if we ask people to tell us what they are thinking about when they solve, say, an algebra problem, we have not only their comments about what they are doing but also the partial working and final results of their calculations, which can be used to verify their comments on what they were thinking about at different steps through the solution. Ericsson and Simon admit that the accuracy of a verbal protocol can be affected by the nature of the task. A high level of reliability is achieved when subjects report the current contents of short-term memory, rather than base the report on information stored in long-term memory which can be distorted by other stored knowledge. This means that accuracy of reporting is highest when it occurs at the same time; that is, is concurrent with the task rather than retrospectively. It is also important that the amount of prompting by the experimenter is minimized. The performance of subjects on problem-solving tasks with and without concurrent reporting was compared by Ericsson and Simon; they concluded from their findings that giving verbal protocols does not significantly influence the subjects' performances in most instances.

What other factors might influence the accuracy of verbal protocols? Some of the cognitive processes underlying problem solving will be 'automatic' and, by definition, unconscious and so will not be open to introspection. 'Pattern recognition processes' are automatic, for example, and we wouldn't expect subjects to be able to talk about such processes. The best we can hope for is information in a subject's statements that permits us to infer that particular mental processes occur in a given task situation.

Summary of Section 6

- Cognitive psychologists, like other scientists, make heavy use of controlled experiments in order to determine which of a myriad of proposed factors have some influence on behaviour in given circumstances. The main idea is to keep all factors constant (e.g. age, amount of experience, IQ, etc.) except the one or two under investigation (e.g. duration of presentation of stimulus material, type of stimulus material, etc.); the factors under investigation are allowed to vary in a controlled manner.
- Computer simulation demonstrates how a problem *could* be solved. The main advantage of computer models of problem solving is that they are highly specific, detailed and explicit.
- Verbal protocols are used to externalize a subject's internal problem-solving strategies. Although verbal protocols are not a complete record of the internal processes involved in problem solving, they do provide invaluable information about them.

7   *Conclusions*

Cognitive psychologists have gone a long way in developing a scientific basis for studying problem solving. Besides devising methods for classifying problems, they have provided a number of important tools for carrying out problem-solving research. State space analysis provides a tool for characterizing the underlying structure of well-defined problems having relatively small problem spaces, and for comparing the structure of problems having different surface characteristics. Collecting and analysing verbal protocols provides us with invaluable (but problematic) data on ongoing solution processes. Computers have been influential in forcing psychologists to be completely explicit in formulating theories of problem solving, and in providing rigorous tests of such theories.

Early research showed that problem difficulty is a function of: the structure of a problem; characteristics of the human information-processing system; previous experience; the strategy employed in solving a problem; and even the way the problem is presented. Problem solving was described as a search in problem spaces. Means-ends analysis was shown to be one powerful general method for guiding a search for solutions to transformation problems.

The toy-world problems that received most attention were very well-defined and required little knowledge for their solution. Although a great deal was learned about problem solving on such problems, it had yet to be shown that the same methods could be used to analyse and understand problem solving in messier, real-world problem-solving situations. As a result, many researchers began to study problem solving in the more complex environments of school and university classrooms. This part of the story will be taken up in Part II.

Much early research was concerned with the conditions under which transfer of learning occurred, or failed to occur. A recurrent and intriguing finding was that although people benefit from repeated experience with the same problem, they often have great difficulty in transferring learning from one problem to different, but closely related problems. Findings such as these led some psychologists to explore the nature of transfer processes. We shall also discuss the beginnings of this research in Part II.

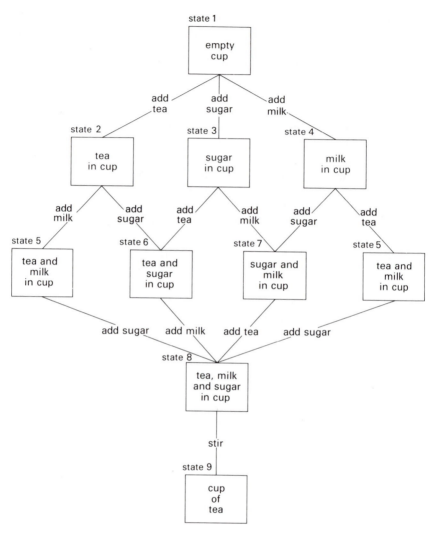

Answer to Activity 3

Part II
Analogical Problem Solving and the Development of Expertise

Contents

1 *Analogical problem solving*

A friend of mine has been keeping a catalogue of the ordinary, everyday-life events his young son understands through analogy. In one example, the child was watching his father cut the grass. The child said that it was like the grass getting a haircut. Of course, this is a nice way of understanding grass cutting, because the child would be able to think about grass cutting in terms of what he already knew about having his hair cut. For example, getting your hair cut can be itchy, irritating and eventually boring, but your hair doesn't seem to suffer much — your hair doesn't hurt while it's being cut. Perhaps the grass doesn't feel anything either (although the ground might get 'irritated'). Maybe it just keeps growing back, like hair. What's underground? A limitless supply of grass? Does a head contain a limitless supply of hair that just keeps pushing its way out? What would happen if somebody cut your hair with a lawnmower, or the grass with a pair of scissors? Is there something beyond the *functional* similarity of the cutting implements that should be taken into consideration?

It could be argued, as Gentner and Gentner (1980) have pointed out, that people don't really use knowledge about one type of event (getting your hair cut) in *reasoning* about a different type of event (cutting the grass). It is possible that reasoning about an event such as cutting the grass occurs independently of any knowledge of analogous events, but that the analogous event provides a convenient framework for talking about the reasoning. That people actively use old knowledge in trying to understand new events or problems has been convincingly and elegantly shown in an experiment carried out by Gentner and Gentner (1980). The experiment involved two groups of subjects. One group was told that the flow of electricity could be understood in terms of the movement of crowds in a place like Euston station, and that a resistor was like a turnstile through which only one person could pass at a time. The other group was told the flow of electricity could be understood in terms of the flow of water through pipes, and that a resistor could be thought of as a 'skinny' section of pipe, which produces a drop in water flow. Gentner and Gentner presented the two groups of subjects with a problem in understanding the effect of a pair of resistors on the flow of electricity through a system. The voltage in an electrical system changes when a current passes through a resistor. The effect of a *pair* of resistors depends on the way in which the resistors are connected. If the resistors are connected in a series (that is, one after the other), the total effect is a drop in voltage, by comparison with a single resistor.

However, if resistors are connected in parallel (that is, side by side), then a greater current flow occurs than would occur given a single resistor. Gentner and Gentner argued that subjects given the water pipe analogy would predict that voltage would drop in all situations involving resistors, because they would think of resistors (skinny sections of pipe) as an impediment to water flow. They predicted that subjects given the moving crowds analogy should do better because they would think of two turnstiles (resistors) connected in parallel as facilitating the movement of people, while two turnstiles connected in series would slow people down more than a single turnstile would. The results showed that the answers given by the two groups of subjects could be predicted by the model of electricity flow they had previously been taught. These findings suggest that people do interpret a new problem in terms of what they know already. The general term for the use of problem strategies derived from experience with similar problems is *analogical problem solving*. The idea is that people solve problems by identifying analogies between old problems (hair cutting) and new problems (lawn mowing). This is another example of the *transfer* of past experience with one type of problem to another; for example, between the Towers of Hanoi and the Chinese Tea Ceremony problems.

1.1   Ill-defined problems

All of the research on the transfer of learning discussed in Part I was concerned with well-defined transformation problems in which the initial and goal states and legal operators are clearly defined. This meant that identities between the solution to *isomorphic* problems (for example, Towers of Hanoi or the Chinese Tea Ceremony) and similarities between *homomorphic* problems (for example, Missionaries and Cannibals and Jealous Husbands) could be easily identified. In this section I shall describe recent research on ill-defined problems where it is not always clear what the problem is, much less the solution. An ill-defined problem is one that lacks clear details of the initial or goal states, or which does not include a complete specification of the operators (moves) that can be employed in solving the problem. Research on such problems brings the analysis of problem solving much closer to our everyday concerns.

Since you have not yet had an opportunity to analyse an ill-defined problem, I shall begin by presenting you with details of what I shall call the 'fortress' problem.

Activity 8

The *fortress problem* tells a story about a general who wanted to rid his country of a tyrant. You should read the story all the way through at least once, and then answer the SAQs that follow, referring back to the story as often as you want. It is very important for you to attempt both SAQs because the experience will make it a lot easier for you to follow the discussion in the following sections.

A small country fell under the iron rule of a dictator. The dictator ruled the country from a strong fortress. The fortress was situated in the middle of the country, surrounded by farms and villages. Many roads radiated outward from the fortress like the spokes on a wheel. A great general raised a large army at the border, vowing to capture the fortress and free the country of the dictator. The general knew that if his entire army could attack the fortress at once it could be captured. His troops were poised at the head of one of the roads leading to the fortress, ready to attack. However, a spy brought the general a disturbing report. The ruthless dictator had planted mines on each of the roads. The mines were set so that small bodies of men could pass over them safely, since the dictator needed to be able to move troops and workers to and from the fortress. However, any large force would detonate the mines. Not only would this blow up the road and render it impassable, but the dictator would then destroy many villages in retaliation. A full-scale direct attack on the fortress therefore appeared impossible.

The general, however, was undaunted. He divided his army up into small groups and dispatched each group to the head of a different road. When all was ready he gave the signal, and each group charged down a different road. All of the small groups passed safely over the mines, and the army then attacked the fortress in full strength. In this way the general was able to capture the fortress and overthrow the dictator.

SAQ 9
Referring back to the text of the fortress problem, fill in the details for each of the following. *Hint*: The first paragraph of the fortress problem story contains the details of the problem, and the second paragraph contains the solution. So all the information you need to answer this SAQ is contained in the first paragraph.
Initial state:
Goal state:
Operators:
Operator restrictions:

SAQ 10
In what sense is the fortress problem ill-defined?

1.2   Duncker's 'radiation' problem

In early studies of problem solving on 'practical problems', Duncker, the famous Gestalt psychologist, made extensive use of the 'radiation' problem (see below). Duncker was a very early exponent of verbal protocols. In his experiments (Duncker, 1945) he asked subjects to read the radiation problem and then to try to think of as many solutions to the problem as they could. They were encouraged to use pencil and paper and to draw figures or make any notes they wished, and were asked to speak aloud anything at all that came into their minds.

Activity 9

Try to solve the *radiation problem* before reading further. Get some paper and a pencil and write down as many possible solutions as you can think of. Even if you can think immediately of reasons why a possible solution should be rejected, write it down. Spend at least five minutes solving it.

> Suppose you are a doctor faced with a patient who has a malignant tumour in his stomach. It is impossible to operate on the patient, but unless the tumour is destroyed the patient will die. There is a kind of ray that can be used to destroy the tumour. If the rays reach the tumour all at once with sufficiently high intensity, the tumour will be destroyed. Unfortunately at this intensity the healthy tissue that the rays pass through on the way to the tumour will also be destroyed. At lower intensities the rays are harmless to healthy tissue, but they will not affect the tumour either. What type of procedure might be used to destroy the tumour with the rays, and at the same time avoid destroying the healthy tissues?

SAQ 11
Using the text of the radiation problem, specify each of the following:
Initial state:
Goal state:
Operators:
Operator restrictions:

SAQ 12
In what sense is the radiation problem ill-defined? Now try to think of other possible solutions to the radiation problem.

The initial and goal states in the radiation problem are well-defined, as are the restrictions on the use of any operators that might be used to solve the problem. The operator restrictions disallow surgery or any physical action that would destroy healthy tissue. Nevertheless, the problem as a whole is ill-defined because the possible operators are specified only very generally: *use rays* to destroy the tumour. In order to solve the problem an operator must be transformed into something a lot more specific: that is, *how* to use the rays to destroy the tumour without destroying healthy tissues.

One way you yourself might have solved the radiation problem was to use what you knew about the solution to the fortress problem as a framework for thinking about how to use the special rays to destroy the patient's stomach tumour. This solution involves 'dividing the rays' and directing numerous applications of low intensity rays at the tumour simultaneously — analogous to the general's solution which involved dividing an army and sending numerous small units along the many roads radiating out from the fortress. If you did this, you solved the tumour problem by applying an analogy from the fortress problem. In fact, you have just taken part in an informal experiment; an experiment similar in spirit to an experiment performed by Gick and Holyoak (1980) to investigate analogical problem solving.

1.3   Gick and Holyoak's transfer experiments

In this section I shall describe two of the many experiments conducted by Gick and Holyoak. In Experiment 1, Gick and Holyoak investigated subjects' ability to solve problems by analogy when they were given a hint to do so, and in Experiment 3 they investigated subjects' ability to notice spontaneously an analogy. The details of these experiments are presented in Techniques Boxes B and C.

TECHNIQUES BOX B

Gick and Holyoak (1980)
Experiment 1

Rationale
Gick and Holyoak set out to discover whether subjects could use analogies in solving the radiation problem if they were given a hint to do so. The experimenters devised a number of story analogies that differed in the type of solution suggested. Gick and Holyoak predicted that subjects would be significantly influenced by the type of solution presented in the particular story analogy they were asked to read before solving the radiation problem.

Method
Gick and Holyoak informed their subjects that the experiment was in two parts. One group (the control group) was simply asked to solve the radiation problem. For the three experimental groups, the first part of the experiment was presented as a memory recall task, in which subjects would be presented with a *story* (actually a version of the fortress problem), and their task would be to summarize the story. All of the story analogies contained exactly the same first paragraph (the first paragraph of the fortress story presented in Activity 8), but differed according to the solution presented in the

---

63

second paragraph. In one version (called the Tunnel story; see Table 2.1) the general dug a tunnel to the fort. In another version (called the Open Supply Route story), the general used one of the main roads to the fortress, which he knew the tyrant kept open as a supply route. The third version was called the Attack-Dispersion story, and contained the disperse-and-converge solution with which you are familiar from Activity 8.

Table 2.1

---

(1) Control group: No story → Radiation problem
(2) Experimental Group 1: Tunnel story → Radiation problem
(3) Experimental Group 2: Open Supply story → Radiation problem
(4) Experimental Group 3: Attack-Dispersion story → Radiation problem

---

All four groups of subjects were informed that the second part of the experiment involved a problem-solving task. In this part of the experiment they would be presented with a problem and asked to report as many possible solutions as they could think of. They were told that in solving the radiation problem they should try to use the story problem they had already read and summarized (i.e. they were given a hint). Subjects were allowed to re-read the story analogy whenever they wished. They were asked to provide 'think aloud' verbal protocols as they were solving the problem.

Results
All subjects who had been given the Attack-Dispersion version of the fortress problem proposed a disperse-and-converge solution to the radiation problem. This solution was proposed by only 10 per cent of the subjects who had received the Open Supply Route story, 20 per cent of subjects who had received the Tunnel story, and one of the control subjects. 70 per cent of subjects who had been given the Open Route story proposed 'open passage' solutions (for example, sending high-intensity rays down the oesophagus), significantly more than any of the other groups. 80 per cent of subjects who had received the Tunnel story suggested operating on the patient.

The results of Experiment 1 showed that subjects were very good at employing an analogy when they were told to do so. The results also showed that the nature of the prior analog story had a significant determining effect on the kind of solution that was proposed for the radiation problem. In all conditions, the most frequent solution was that suggested by the story analogy that subjects had been given in the first part of the experiment.

TECHNIQUES BOX C

Gick and Holyoak (1980)
Experiment 3

Rationale
This experiment was designed to investigate analogical problem solving in more realistic conditions than those in which previous experiments had been conducted. In everyday situations, people may not be given a hint to use an analogy in solving a problem. Also, when solving problems by analogy people have to search memory for a relevant analog problem.

Method
As in Experiment 1, subjects were told that the first part of the experiment involved a memory recall task and the second part involved a problem-solving task. Two groups of subjects were presented with the version of the fortress problem story that contained the disperse-and-converge solution, plus two other stories that were completely disanalogous to the radiation problem (see Table 2.2 for a summary of the experimental design). The fortress problem story was the second story presented to both groups. Subjects were asked to read the stories and to recall them in as much detail as possible. Both groups were then asked to find as many solutions as they could to the radiation problem. The only difference between the two groups was that one group was given the following hint: 'In solving this problem you may find that one of the stories you read before will give you a hint for a solution of this problem.' The other group received no hint.

Table 2.2

Group 1: Story 1 → Story 2 → Story 3 → Hint → Radiation
        problem
Group 2: Story 1 → Story 2 → Story 3 → No hint → Radiation
        problem

Results
92 per cent of subjects in the hint condition proposed the disperse-and-converge solution to the radiation problem, whereas only 20 per cent of the subjects in the no hint condition proposed this solution.

In the 'no hint' condition of Experiment 3, Gick and Holyoak were trying to lead their subjects to believe that the two parts of the experiment were unrelated so that they could investigate whether or not subjects would recognize spontaneously that information acquired in the first part was relevant to the problem presented in the second part of the experiment. Story 1 and Story 3 were included so as to disguise the relevance of the fortress story with the disperse-and-converge solution.

When I introduced you to the fortress problem I presented it under the pretext of giving you a chance to analyse an ill-defined problem, but my real purpose was to give you an opportunity to experience for yourself the kind of situation Gick and Holyoak's subjects faced. I don't know whether or not you perceived the relationship between the fortress and radiation problems, but Gick and Holyoak's results showed that subjects were quite good at employing knowledge of the fortress problem and its solution when solving the radiation problem *only* if the experimenter gave them a hint that the problems were related. If subjects were not given a hint — as was the case in my informal experiment — the analogy was not so helpful.

SAQ 13
In Section 4.1 of Part 1, I discussed research by Reed *et al.* on transfer between the Missionaries and Cannibals and Jealous Husbands problems. How are Gick and Holyoak's findings related to the findings of Reed *et al.*?

In another experiment, Gick and Holyoak presented the fortress story *after* subjects had already begun work on the radiation problem. In this experiment subjects were informed that the experimenters were interested in 'incubation' phenomena (that is, the effects of taking time off from solution attempts and doing a different task for a while.) The subjects were asked to work on a problem (the radiation problem) for a period of time, after which they would be given the fortress story to read as a filler task. Even in this condition, most subjects still failed to recognize the fortress story as analogous to the radiation problem unless they were given a hint. I tried in SAQ 12 to replicate the 'hint' condition of Gick and Holyoak's experiments by asking you to think about the problem again after you had answered SAQs 9–12, the answers to which were intended to demonstrate the similarities between the two problems.

If it seems incredible to you that Gick and Holyoak's subjects failed to notice the analogy between the fortress and radiation problems, even when the fortress problem was introduced while subjects were attempting to solve the radiation problem, consider the following situation. Imagine that you are a student taking two different types of course during a certain academic year; for the sake of argument, Philosophy and Introductory Psychology. At the end of the year, it turns out that both of your examinations are to be held on the same day. You sit your Philosophy examination in the morning and the Psychology examination in the afternoon. (You do not need to have taken a course in either subject in order to follow the point I want to make.) During the Philosophy examination you answer the following question:

> If asked to describe 'reality' would you base your description on existentialist or realist philosophy? Justify your choice.

In the afternoon, you find the following among the questions on the Introductory Psychology examination paper:

> If you knew someone who needed treatment for a neurotic condition, would you recommend behaviour modification or psycho-analysis? Why?

Now imagine that you consider answering this second question. But you start daydreaming a bit, thinking about the Philosophy examination, wondering how well you performed, even briefly reviewing your answer to the question you attempted. Do you think you would have seen a connection between your current problem and your answer to the question about the nature of reality?

You could be forgiven for thinking that these examination questions are unrelated, that your answer to the Philosophy question would not help you in answering the Psychology question. But, in fact, both questions are of a *type* in which the examinee is being asked to compare and contrast, and to evaluate, different ideas on the one hand, and treatment methods on the other. If you had devoted a lot of time to organizing an answer to a question of this type on the Philosophy paper, then the organization of the answer might well serve as a framework for answering the question on the Psychology paper. The subjects in Gick and Holyoak's experiments, where the fortress story was presented in the context of a 'memory task', and the radiation story in the context of a 'problem-solving task', were in much the same situation as a person sitting examinations in unrelated fields. In both situations, it is exceedingly difficult to perceive the connection between events where the relationship is buried under a lot of surface dissimilarities.

Summary of Section 1

- People often understand and talk about events, including their own problem-solving behaviour, using their knowledge of analogous events as a framework.
- Gentner and Gentner have shown that people can also solve problems by applying the knowledge they derived when learning about similar problems. This is known as analogical problem-solving abilities or learning.

- In this section you were presented with two ill-defined problems: the first was accompanied by its solution, and you were asked to solve the second. The solution involved transforming a quite general statement of operators into specific actions that could be performed to achieve the goal of the second problem.
- Gick and Holyoak have carried out a series of experiments investigating the solving of an ill-defined problem, where an analogical problem and solution were also presented. They repeatedly found that the vast majority of their subjects used the analogy to solve the current problem only when they were given a hint that the two problems were related.
- Gick and Holyoak also found that the vast majority of subjects could successfully use the solution to a previous problem in solving an analogous problem once they were given a hint to do so.

2 Representations of knowledge

Gick and Holyoak suggest that analogical problem solving is an especially useful heuristic in situations that people find somewhat novel. The radiation problem is novel for most people because they know very little about medical procedures or about 'rays' or about whether 'rays' can be 'divided'. Faced with such a problem, a very useful strategy would involve searching memory for an analogous situation. If an analogous situation were found, then its solution might serve as a framework for thinking about a solution to the current problem.

A prerequisite of analogical problem solving is that there should be a mental representation in memory of an analogous problem. Gick and Holyoak, borrowing terms from Gentner (1979), call the previously experienced problem the *base problem* and the current problem the *target problem*. One of the important issues in analogical problem-solving research is to understand how the description of the current target problem is used in searching long-term memory for a base problem. It is assumed that the target problem is represented in short-term *working memory* and the analogous *base problem* is represented in *long-term memory*. The difficulty, then, becomes one of *memory retrieval*: in other words, the retrieval of a problem which is analogous to the current problem. If a person succeeds in retrieving an analogous problem from long-term memory, for example the fortress problem, this will result in positive transfer to the new problem; if not, the new problem (for example, the radiation problem) will have to be tackled from scratch. (It is also possible for an old problem solution to be retrieved which is in fact a *false analogy*. False analogies can lead to incorrect solutions: for example, assuming that because you have met

one ferocious redheaded person, all redhaired people are quick tem-
pered, leading to an inappropriate solution to the problem of reacting
to redheaded strangers.)

To see why finding a good analogy is a difficult matter, compare the
representations of the fortress and radiation problems, which were given
in the answers to SAQs 9 and 11, and which are also presented in
Table 2.3.

Table 2.3

(a) Long-term memory Base problem (fortress)	(b) Working memory Target problem (radiation)
INITIAL STATE: General outside fortress with army. Tyrant inside fortress. Roads radiating out from the fortress have been mined. Large bodies of men passing along a road would set off the mines, destroying the roads and making them impassable. If the roads are destroyed, the tyrant would destroy many villages in retaliation.	*INITIAL STATE*: Tumour in patient's stomach. Doctor is not allowed to operate. Doctor has special ray which can be used for treatment. High intensity rays destroy healthy tissues as well as tumours. Low intensity rays neither destroy tumours nor damage healthy tissues.
GOAL: General overthrows tyrant.	*GOAL*: Doctor destroys tumour.
OPERATORS: General can use army to attack fortress.	*OPERATORS*: Doctor can use special rays to destroy tumour.
RESTRICTIONS: General must avoid destruction of army and villages.	*RESTRICTIONS*: Doctor must avoid damage to healthy tissue.
SOLUTION: General divides army into small units. General sends units down the many roads radiating out from the fortress. General reassembles army at fortress. Army attacks fortress in strength.	*SOLUTION*: ?????

The striking thing about these representations is that they have
nothing in common 'on the surface'. In the one case, the objects represented are things such as a hospital patient, a doctor, special rays,
and so forth. In the other, the objects are a dictator and a general,
armies, mines, roads and villages. So there is a difficulty in explaining
how the mind is able to find correspondences between events which
are, on the face of it, completely unrelated.

2.1 Levels of abstraction

Gick and Holyoak make the point that stories or problems can be represented at many different *levels of abstraction*. At a surface level of abstraction the fortress and radiation stories would contain the different details actually presented in the stories. At a deeper level of abstraction, though, both stories could be described in terms of someone having the *goal* of 'overcoming an obstacle'. Since there are few — if any — correspondences between the two problems at the surface level of description (generals and doctors, and so on), Gick and Holyoak argue that the process of being reminded of one problem in the presence of the other must be mediated through deep-level abstractions of the two problems which reveal their similarities.

Kintsch and Van Dijk (1978) proposed a theory of how memory representations are structured in long-term memory (see Greene, 1986). They suggested that *memory structures* are constructed from experience as a result of abstracting the essential content, or 'gist' of a situation. Kintsch and Van Dijk have proposed a number of processes for constructing abstract representations of the events we hear or read about, including deletion, generalization and construction. In order to see how these processes are thought to work, consider the first three sentences of the fortress story:

> A small country fell under the iron rule of a dictator. The dictator ruled the country from a strong fortress. The fortress was situated in the middle of the country.

A concrete surface representation of this story would contain most of the details of the story. A slightly more abstract representation could be created by the *deletion process* which removes inessential details from the surface-level description. Deletion reduces the amount of information in the structure of a memory representation, but preserves the 'gist' of the story. Applied to the first three lines of the fortress story, deletion would result in the following representation:

> A country was ruled by a dictator. The dictator ruled from a fortress in the middle of the country.

Even more abstract levels of representation could be achieved by making successive deletions. If the deletion process were applied again, this time to the second-level abstraction, we might have:

> A fortress was located in the centre of the country.

The *generalization process* also reduces the amount of information in a memory structure. An example of generalization would be the transformation of a great deal of detailed information in the text about the 'planting of mines', the 'resultant danger to troops and villages', and 'the general's plan of attack' into a more abstract description such as: 'the general wanted to prevent widespread destruction'.

The *construction process* adds information rather than reduces it. Construction involves making inferences about events and motivations which are implied rather than stated directly. In psychology, inferences are often defined as 'going beyond' what is actually present in a story or problem situation. Understanding often involves the ability to attribute causes to the actions people perform. For example, nowhere in the fortress story is it directly stated that the *reason* the tyrant planted mines in the roads was to prevent an attack on his fortress by a large army. Nor does the story state why the general divided his army and sent small units down all the roads converging on the fortress. But most people automatically infer that his reasons were that he did not want to have his army destroyed and he did want to protect the villages. Construction processes often involve adding information to a representation in terms of inferred causal relations and intentions; that is, the goals that can be attributed to actors in order to explain sequences of actions.

SAQ 14
Here are two little stories:
1 Debbie told Judy that John was back in London. That night, Judy moved to Sheffield.
2 As George rounded the corner he saw a police car sitting in front of his house. He did an about-turn and quickly walked away.
(a) What would you say is the common causal relation between the pair of events described in the two different stories? *Hint*: What goal is shared by Judy and George?
(b) On a scale from 1 to 10, how similar are these two stories 'on the surface'?
(c) On a scale from 1 to 10, how similar are these two stories in terms of the causal relation you identified in (a)?

When causal relations are made explicit, the similarities between seemingly different events become somewhat more transparent. A memory retrieval search would have less difficulty matching abstract descriptions that reveal similarities between two representations than it would have matching the surface-level representations involving the specific details of the two problems. However, one major difficulty with hypothesizing 'abstraction processes' like Kintsch and Van Dijk's is that at the deepest level of abstraction all problems might seem to be analogous. For instance, at the deepest level of abstraction, the radiation and fortress problems could both be described as follows: *somebody did something to achieve something*. The same description would also apply to a story about somebody stealing a car to get to an appointment on time, or to any other story about someone performing some act in order to achieve some goal, although those analogies would not be helpful. Perceptions of the relationship between two representations depend upon the level of abstraction at which they are matched. At intermediate levels, many similarities will be apparent, but not all of the irrelevant differences will have been abstracted. Gick and Holyoak argue that the *optimal level of abstraction* is that at which the similarities between two representations are maximized, and differences minimized. This optimum level would correspond to an intermediate level of abstraction. At the deepest level there is too much similarity; at the surface level, too little.

The importance of research into memory retrieval processes for understanding problem-solving behaviour is highlighted by Gick and Holyoak's finding that subjects often fail to notice spontaneously the relationship between a current problem and stored knowledge. Advances in our understanding of memory storage and retrieval processes would do a lot to enhance our understanding of analogical transfer of solutions between problems.

2.2 Applying old solutions to new problems

So far we have been talking about how problems are represented in memory in a way that allows a new problem to be analysed and re-cognized as similar or different. But naturally the purpose of all this is that the solutions to earlier problems can be used to help the problem solver to adapt them to solve the new problem. In the problem representations given in Table 2.3, the representation of the fortress problem contains 'solution' information. But the problem is how the solution to this problem can be transformed into a solution for the analogous radiation problem. Assuming that a person has recognized that the fortress and radiation problems are related (through being given a hint, say), we would still be faced with the problem of how the solution to the fortress problem (dividing and reassembling an army) could be translated into a solution to the radiation problem (convergence of low intensity rays directed at the tumour from a number of different sources).

Duncker (1945) suggested that problem solving involved both problem solution processes and problem reformulation processes in turns. According to this theory, a person would solve, or partially solve, one part of a problem and then use the solution as a means of redefining what the problem is. With this new, somewhat clearer perspective on the problem, problem solving would again be initiated. Gick and Holyoak investigated their subjects' strategies for solving the radiation problem by evaluating their verbal protocols. Like Duncker, they found that some subjects arrived at a solution only after trying out and rejecting or modifying partial solutions. They called this process of refining solutions *solution development*.

2.3 Solution development

In order to demonstrate the process of gradual development of a solution, consider the progress of one of Gick and Holyoak's subjects, called S15 (subject number 15). S15 had been presented with the fortress story before attempting the radiation problem. Relevant extracts from the subject's verbal protocol as she was trying to solve the radiation problem are presented in Table 2.4. The single comment made by the experimenter is preceded by '(X)' in the table.

I have divided the protocol into seven different segments, labelled (a), (b), (c), (d), (e), (f) and (X), in order to make my discussion easier to follow. Altogether S15 generated three possible solutions to the problem — in the segments marked (a), (b) and (d) in Table 2.4.

Table 2.4 Extract from protocol of S15 in Gick and Holyoak's experiment (adapted from Gick and Holyoak, 1980)

Subject reads radiation problem.
(a) 'Alright I, what I most, what I'd probably do is send the ray at sufficiently high intensity and then take the risk that the tissues, the healthy tissues that would be destroyed, could be repaired later on.'
(b) 'Trying to relate this to the other problem, I could say that you could give multiple treatments of low-intensity ray. But from this problem it seems that they won't have an effect on the tumour ... So I don't think that would work.'
    Later ...
(c) 'Alright, in that way my first suggestion would probably not be the way to go at it. Because that way you're getting low intensity so it won't destroy the tissue and hopefully over a period of time the additive effect of low intensity rays would kill the tumour. But from reading the article, I don't know if that would work or not, because it says that a low intensity ray doesn't have any effect on the tumour at all. So I don't know. I don't know any other possible ways of doing it.'

(X) *'Would it help to possibly go back to the story and see whether you can apply that?'*

(d) 'Well, that's what I was trying to do here. It says here he divides his army into different small groups. Okay, ... possibly. What they could do, but this is a whole new solution now, possibly what they could do is attack the tumour from a multiple of directions, with low intensity rays ...
(e) and then, since you're coming in from all different directions ... with small intensity rays you're not going to be destroying the healthy tissue but ...
(f) they'll all converge at the point of the tumour which will hopefully destroy the tumour.'

S15's first solution was simply to blast the tumour with high intensity rays and to repair any damage done to healthy tissues later. S15 announced her second proposed solution, (b), immediately after presenting this first solution. I presume that S15 realized that her first solution was not acceptable under the rules of the problem.

S15's second solution involved the application of a succession of low intensity rays to the tumour. Unfortunately, the protocol contains no information to indicate where these ideas came from. However, this solution has important elements (for example, weak rays) of the third solution, and as such appears to be an intermediate step towards the next and last solution. S15's reason for rejecting her second solution is that weak rays applied over time would not accumulate sufficient intensity to destroy the tumour. S15 arrived at the 'dispersion' solution of sending many weak rays simultaneously, (d), after prompting by the experimenter. At (e) and (f) the subject evaluates the solution with respect to the operator restrictions ('with small intensity rays you're not going to be destroying the healthy tissue') and the goal state ('they'll all converge at the point of the tumour which will hopefully destroy the tumour').

Activity 10
Re-read the protocol segments marked (X) and (d) in Table 2.4. What evidence is there that subject S15 relied on an abstract stored representation of the fortress story as a framework for thinking about and solving the radiation problem?

In fact, the protocol evidence indicates that S15 is not relying on a stored memory representation of the fortress problem at all, but is actually working out her solution by referring directly to the text of the fortress problem. Remember, though, that the point of the analysis is to try to gain some insight into the way analogical problem solving might work, given that we have no information to work with when people 'automatically' generate an analogous solution to a problem.

Protocol evidence such as we have been discussing adds plausibility to Gick and Holyoak's suggestion that analogical problem solving involves the construction of a series of solutions, each of which is an outgrowth of the previous solution. Moreover, each partial solution to a problem can serve as a retrieval cue for related information in memory. When related information is retrieved, it can be used as a framework in which to modify the most recent solution. The result would be a somewhat transformed solution that, in its turn, would serve as the next retrieval cue, and so on.

2.4   Problem-solving schemas

One significant aspect of the transformation from novice to expert in any domain of learning is the acquisition of problem-solving schemas. *Problem-solving schemas* are memory representations which embody knowledge based on past experiences with a particular type of problem. The process of constructing such a representation is also called *schema learning*. Gick and Holyoak (1983) conducted a series of experiments to investigate the conditions under which *schema learning* is most likely to occur. In some of these experiments Gick and Holyoak measured the effects of teaching a schema for 'convergence problems' more or less directly. For example, in one experiment they presented a group of subjects with a prior story analog, such as the fortress problem, plus a statement of the abstract principle underlying the solution to convergence problems: 'If you need a large force to accomplish some purpose, but are prevented from applying such a force directly, many smaller forces applied simultaneously from different directions may work just as well.' In a second condition, only the abstract principle was given before the radiation problem. In a third condition, the fortress problem alone was presented before the radiation problem. When Gick and Holyoak compared the number of analogous solutions in all conditions, both before and after a hint was given, they found that presenting an explicit statement of important aspects of the schema for convergence problems was no help at all. In fact, there was no difference in performance among the different conditions either before or after the hint.

Gick and Holyoak found that subjects were far more likely to acquire a problem schema if two prior analog stories were presented, instead of just one. For example, subjects were presented with both the fortress problem and a story about a fire at an oil rig. The firefighters had a vast quantity of fire retardant foam at their disposal, but they did not have a hose large enough to put a large quantity of foam on the fire quickly. The solution (you've guessed it) involved stationing a number of firefighters around the oil rig with all the small hoses that were available. Subjects were asked to read and summarize each story, and also to compare and contrast the stories, which they were allowed to re-read as and when they wanted. In this situation subjects were about twice as likely to generate an analogous solution to the radiation problem as a group of subjects who were asked to compare and contrast either the fortress problem or the firefighting problem with a second, non-analogous story. In another experiment, Gick and Holyoak found even larger transfer effects when subjects were provided with two prior analog stories plus a statement of the solution principle common to both.

Another line of research has explored Gick and Holyoak's assumptions about the role of schemas in facilitating transfer. Gick and Holyoak assume that possession of a schema facilitates transfer to new problems because a schema makes it easier to access information relevant to solution of the current problem. The reason for this is that schema acquisition involves the elimination of differences between problems belonging to the same class, and summarization of common features. Acquiring a schema is equivalent to constructing a representation of the optimum level of abstraction (see Section 2.1 above). A new problem should have more features in common with the schema than with any particular prior example problem. As a result, the schema will be retrieved when a new problem is presented and its solution procedure made available for use in the context of the new problem. This is known as *automatic abstraction*.

This idea has been applied to student learning in a number of different domains. However, the automatic abstraction view doesn't really take into account the fact that initial learning may lead to as many misconceptions as insights: that is, the notion that students have a mental representation (a schema) that accurately reflects the concepts and procedures which are currently being acquired is a fiction. When students look back at an exercise problem, they may or may not understand what the exercise problem is about; they may or may not understand the solution even if they know what the problem is. An example would be a student learning computer programming who says, 'I know this is a recursion problem, but I can't understand recursion for the life of me. I just can't understand how recursion works'.

This issue has been highlighted in research conducted by Brown and Clement (1989) who devised techniques for presenting *bridging analogies* to help students overcome misconceptions. Bridging analogies function like Gick and Holyoak's hints, but are more elaborate. Brown and Clement argue that bridging analogies may be necessary when a particular analogy used for teaching purposes fails. The purpose of the bridging analogy is to help the student make a connection between the current problem and the training analogy which proved to be no help at all.

An example from Brown and Clement is the case where a student cannot understand that a table exerts an upward influence on a book resting on the table (which, of course, it does). So the teacher suggests that the student think of a book resting on a spring. In this situation the student agrees that the spring is exerting an upward influence on the book, but says this is because the spring has been compressed by the book and 'the spring wants to return to its original position'. But the student still insists that this cannot be the case with the table because the table is rigid and therefore has no original other position to return to. At this point, a bridging analogy would be presented, in which the student is invited to consider a book resting on a flexible board between two supports. This is a useful analogy connecting the original analogous situations. The bridging analogy is like the book on a spring problem, in that the book on the flexible board bends the board, though less pronouncedly, and it leads the student to understand that a table top could be conceived of as a board that also bends, though imperceptibly.

Brown and Clement argue for a different conception of what it is about analogies that facilitates transfer from one problem to another. Although they do not claim that abstractions are unimportant in analogical transfer, they argue that in many cases the exact opposite — a concrete model of a situation — may be the only way to help students conceptualize correspondences between problems that seem very different on the surface. In effect, Brown and Clement extend the range of analogical problem-solving processes that may be available to people in learning situations, or that may be taught in such situations.

Summary of Section 2

- In analogical problem solving the current target problem, as it is represented in short-term working memory, is used to retrieve a representation of a previously experienced base problem from long-term memory.
- Gick and Holyoak suggest that, for a helpful analogy to be retrieved, the target and base problems must be represented at an appropriate level of abstraction. While there may be few correspondences between the surface-level details of two different problems, deeper-level abstractions may reveal similarities.
- Kintsch and Van Dijk propose that concrete representations of events are made more abstract by three types of process: deletion of inessential details; generalization, by substituting the general categories to which events belong; and construction, by adding inferences, including causal relations.
- If abstraction processes are taken to the deepest level, then all problems are analogous. Gick and Holyoak argue that the optimal level of abstraction is an intermediate one where similarities are maximized and differences are minimized.
- Once an analogy has been recognized and a base problem retrieved from memory, the solution of the base problem must be translated into a solution to the target problem.
- Gick and Holyoak have found that in analogical problem solving subjects may generate and develop a series of partial solutions to the target problem, a process they term solution development. They

suggest that each successive partial solution serves as a framework for modifying the most recent partial solution to produce a new one.

- Gick and Holyoak's experiments suggest that analogical problem solving may not be a useful heuristic in problem solving since the difficulty of analogous problems is often only overcome when a hint is given by the experimenter. However, hints are often more readily available for real-world problems.

- Experience of a number of related problems can result in the acquisition of a problem-solving schema, a general strategy for dealing with a particular type of problem. This process is called schema learning.

- Investigating schema learning, Gick and Holyoak found no difference in the number of analogical solutions produced by groups of subjects receiving one prior analog, or a statement of the abstract solution principle, or both. However, subjects were far more likely to acquire a problem schema if two prior analogs were presented, and even more so if the abstract solution principle was presented as well.

- Brown and Clement argue that concrete models of situations may be as important in analogical problem solving as abstractions (schemas) acquired after considerable experience with a particular type of problem.

3   *Extensions to classroom learning*

Research by Gick and Holyoak helped to renew interest in research into analogical problem solving. In order to understand the importance of such research, consider the way in which students learn from textbooks, particularly in mathematics and the sciences. In a given section of text, definitions will be given for one or two new concepts, and instruction in a new principle or procedure for solving a class of problems will be presented. There is usually a list of exercise problems at the end of the section that provide students with an opportunity to practise whatever it was they were supposed to learn in that section.

It is now well known in problem-solving research that in learning from such textbooks students often refer back to the *example problems* when they are trying to solve *exercise problems* at the end of a section of text (Kahney, 1982; Anderson, Farrell, and Sauers, 1984; Pirolli, 1986). This, of course, is a kind of learning by analogy, since what the student is doing is looking for an example problem which is similar to the current exercise problem. This is not unlike the experimental set-up used by Gick and Holyoak in their research, in which a worked 'example' problem (the fortress problem, for example) was used to make subjects familiar with the solution (disperse-and-converge) to a class of problems, and was then followed by an 'exercise' problem (the radiation problem) in order to examine the effects of presenting the example problem on the solution to the exercise problem. In many textbooks, an example problem (equivalent to a base problem) and an exercise problem (equivalent to a target problem) are often as unalike, on the surface, as the radiation and fortress problems which we've already discussed. The problem for the student, then, would be to find an example problem in the textbook which was analogous to the current exercise problem and to transform the solution of the example problem into a solution to the exercise problem.

Recent research by Reed, Dempster and Ettinger (1985) has been concerned with the nature of problem types and their effect on learning. Reed, Dempster and Ettinger point out that a single problem category may contain different types of problem. They argue that the usefulness of analogy in such domains should depend upon how similar a problem is to a previous problem for which a solution is already known. In algebra, for example, there is a category of problems known as 'distance problems'. Table 2.5 contains three different distance problems which were used in experiments by Reed, Dempster and Ettinger. Also presented in Table 2.5 are the equations appropriate for each of the three problems (don't worry about the details if you are unfamiliar with algebra problems).

Table 2.5

Problem 1 (Practice problem):	Problem 2 (Equivalent problem):	Problem 3 (Similar problem):
A car travelling at a speed of 30 mph left a certain place at 10 am. At 11.30 am, another car departed from the same place at 40 mph and travelled the same route. In how many hours will the second car overtake the first car?	A car travels south at the rate of 30 mph. Two hours later, a second car leaves to overtake the first car using the same route and going at 45 mph. In how many hours will the second car overtake the first car?	A car leaves 3 hours after a large delivery truck but overtakes it by travelling 15 mph faster. If it takes the car 7 hours to reach the delivery truck, find the rate of each vehicle.
Solution equation: $30t = 40(t - 1.5)$	Solution equation: $30t = 45(t - 2)$	Solution equation: $10r = 7(r + 15)$

Problems 1 and 2 can both be solved using the same equation (but with different values for variables such as speed). Since the same equation can be used to solve both problems, Reed, Dempster and Ettinger refer to such problems as 'equivalent' problems. Problem 3 is also a distance problem, but its solution involves a slight modification to the equation that solves Problems 1 and 2 (the minus sign inside the brackets must be changed to a plus sign). Reed, Dempster and Ettinger refer to problems that belong to the same category but are of different types as 'similar' problems.

In one experiment, Reed *et al.* presented one group of subjects with a related practice problem (for example, Problem 1 in Table 2.5) followed by an equivalent problem and then a similar problem (for example, Problems 2 and 3, respectively, in Table 2.5). Another group of subjects was given a practice problem that was not related to the two target problems. In all cases, after the subjects had solved, or attempted to solve the practice problem, and before they were presented with the two target problems, the experimenters showed the subjects the correct solution equation for the practice problem they had been given. Subjects who were given a related practice problem, and solution, were told that the solution should help them solve the two target problems. Nothing was said about the relationship between the practice problem and the target problems to the subjects who were given the unrelated practice problem.

The results were extremely interesting. Initially there appeared to be no difference at all between the groups in the number of correct solutions to the target problems. This suggested that solving a related problem (and being shown a correct solution) did not help in solving either equivalent or similar problems. However, when Reed *et al.* compared the number of correct solution equations generated by the two different groups, they did find a significant difference. The subjects who had been given a related practice problem were far more likely to at least use the correct equation in solving the target problems — but they still had trouble with the equations themselves, as shown by the fact that the overall number of solutions did not differ between the two groups.

In a follow-up experiment, Reed *et al.* showed that memory for solutions is an important limiting factor on performance. In this experiment, two groups of subjects were given related practice problems only, plus two equivalent and similar target problems, but one group was allowed to keep the solution to the practice problem in view while they worked on the target problems, while the other group worked on the target problems only after the solution to the practice problem had been removed. Subjects who were allowed to consult the solution to the practice problem produced significantly more correct solutions to the equivalent target problem. Having the solution in view did not help with similar problems.

The most dramatic improvement in performance on equivalent problems occurred when Reed *et al.* presented subjects with elaborated solutions (i.e. solutions that contained more information about how to map problem features on to solution equations) and allowed the subjects to refer to the solutions while they worked on target problems. Elaboration of the solution also produced considerable transfer, even if subjects were not allowed to refer to the solution while working on the target problems, by comparison with a group of subjects who did not receive an elaborated solution, but considerably less than that produced by the group who were allowed to view the solution in the second part of the experiment. Interestingly, even elaboration did not result in transfer on similar problems. Table 2.6 contains a practice distance problem plus an elaborated solution.

Table 2.6

A car travelling at a speed of 30 mph left a certain place at 10 am. At 11.30 am, another car departed from the same place at 40 mph and travelled the same route. In how many hours will the second car overtake the first car?

Answer: The problem is a distance-rate-time problem in which distance = rate × time

We begin by constructing a table to represent the distance, rate and time for each of the two cars. We want to find how long the second car travels before it overtakes the first car. We let 't' represent the number that we want to find and enter it into the table. The first car then travels $t + \frac{3}{2}$ hr because it left $1\frac{1}{2}$ hours earlier. The rates are 30 mph for the first car and 40 mph for the second car. Notice that the first car must travel at a slower rate if the second car overtakes it. We can now represent the distance each car travels by multipying the rate and the time for each car. These values are shown in the table at the right.

Car	Distance (miles)	Rate (mph)	Time (hr)
First	$30(t + \frac{3}{2})$	30	$t + \frac{3}{2}$
Second	$40 \times t$	40	t

Because both cars have travelled the same distance when the second car overtakes the first, we set the two distances equal to each other:

$$60(t + \tfrac{3}{2}) = 40t$$

Solving for 't' yields the following:

$$30t + 45 = 40t$$
$$45 = 10t$$
$$t = 4.5 \text{ hr}$$

The only condition in which subjects showed transfer from a practice problem to a similar problem occurred when Reed *et al.* presented practice problems which were either slightly more complex than a related, similar target problem, or when the practice and similar target problems were of equal complexity.

Because so much research has shown that students rely heavily on worked-out examples in solving exercise problems, these results have important pedagogical implications. In short, the results suggest that considerable care should be taken in selecting practice problems that are closely related to the example problems used in texts. Solutions to example problems should be available to students, and the principle underlying the solution to a problem should be stated explicitly. (Note that many SAQs include a 'hint' to look at specific material presented earlier in the text, and the answers try to remind of principles, thus providing a means of rehearsal of important information.)

Summary of Section 3
- The type of research carried out by Gick and Holyoak has provided a framework for the experimental study of problem solving in settings such as science learning, mathematics, and computer programming in schools and colleges.
- Reed, Dempster and Ettinger argue that a single problem category may contain different types of problem. Once an analog is recognized, problem difficulty depends both on how similar the target problem is to the solution of a base problem and whether the solution is remembered.

4   *Developing expertise*

One of the attractions of puzzle problems like the Towers of Hanoi was the fact that they were novel problems which assumed no prior learning. Even the study of transfer effects was confined to the transfer of learning from one version of a problem to another. Yet in real life we gradually accumulate experience over many years as part of a learning process. We are all aware of the difference between a novice and an expert, whether driving a car, passing exams, playing chess, or diagnosing medical problems. Recall that in solving problems such as the Towers of Hanoi almost no knowledge beyond that provided by the experimenter is needed; although perhaps you did feel yourself to be more of an 'expert' in tackling such problems by the time you finished Part I. But, of course, in ordinary, mundane situations people bring a lot of previously acquired knowledge to bear both in understanding a problem and in solving it.

As described in Part I, early research viewed problem solving as a search for a solution to a problem in a problem space of alternative moves. Efficient or intelligent search of a problem space was seen to be guided by the application of general problem-solving methods, or heuristics, and a lot of the research carried out in that period, especially research in artificial intelligence, was devoted to discovering the different heuristics that might be useful in guiding search for solutions to problems *in any domain, regardless of content.* One implication of this research was that the more general methods a person had acquired, the better that person would be at solving problems. However, another wave of research, into differences between novices and experts in solving problems in more knowledge-intensive tasks than experimental problems like the Towers of Hanoi, led to the view that something much more specific than general methods subserved problem solving and learning.

Bhaskar and Simon (1977) discussed the extension of problem-solving research to *semantically rich domains*, domains of knowledge in which substantial amounts of prior information are necessary to tackle problems. An example of such a domain is geometry. Problem solving in geometry requires a great deal of domain-specific knowledge which has to be learnt, and in that respect it is a semantically rich domain. But it is also what Larkin (1981) has called a *formal domain*. Formal domains are domains that (a) involve a great deal of knowledge and (b) depend on generally agreed logical principles sufficient to solve problems in that domain.

An example of a domain that is semantically rich but is not a formal domain, according to Larkin's definition, is psychology. In order to see this, all you have to do is listen to a behaviourist and a psychoanalyst arguing about the best way to treat neurotic symptoms. Both have a great deal of knowledge but there are no agreed principles for solving the problem.

Beginning in the late 1970s and continuing to the present day, numerous studies have been conducted into the differences between the problem-solving strategies and knowledge structures of novices and experts in domains as varied as physics, architecture and computer programming. Investigators were able to see clear differences in problem solving between novices, intermediate learners and experts; the next step was to ask how expertise was acquired from prior learning experiences. This was the step that led cognitive psychologists to show an interest in *learning processes*. In contrast to the earlier emphasis on modelling *performance processes*, psychologists are now also concerned with changes in performance that occur as an individual is transformed progressively from a novice to an expert.

4.1   Novices and experts

Research has been carried out in several different domains of knowledge, in all of which it is assumed that there are large differences in knowledge between experts, intermediate learners and novices. In this section we shall discuss the domains of chess, computer programming, and physics.

Chess

In 1973, Chase and Simon reported an interesting series of experiments (Chase and Simon, 1973a; 1973b) in which they investigated the ability of chess players of different abilities to reconstruct positions on a game board after being given a very brief period of time for viewing the board. One of their experiments, the 'memory' experiment was a replication of an experiment first performed by de Groot (1965). This experiment is described in Techniques Box D.

TECHNIQUES BOX D

Chase and Simon's Memory Experiment

Rationale

The basic idea was to see whether acquiring expert knowledge of a domain changes the way the information from that domain is organized in memory.

Method

Chase and Simon presented three subjects — a beginner, a class A player, and a Master — with five 'middle-game' positions (with about twenty-five pieces still remaining on the board) and five 'end-game' positions (with about fourteen pieces still remaining on the board). These were taken from positions in actual games discussed in books on chess. They also presented four 'meaningless' middle-game and end-game positions by randomly rearranging the same number of chess pieces on the board.

Subjects were provided with an empty chessboard and a full set of chess pieces. For each trial they were allowed five seconds to view one of the prepared positions, and then, after the position board had been removed, they were asked to reconstruct the position they had seen on their empty board. If a subject failed to construct the position accurately, their board was cleared, the game position was re-presented, and the subject again attempted to reconstruct the entire position from memory. This procedure was repeated until the whole position was perfectly recalled.

Results

Figure 2.1 presents the results for recall of the middle games and end games. Figure 2.1 shows that on average both the class A player and

---

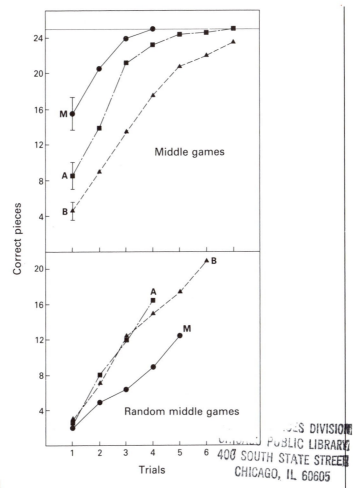

Figure 2.1

the beginner required seven trials to reconstruct middle-game positions, while the Master required only four trials. On end-game
positions (not shown in Figure 2.1) the Master was able to reconstruct
positions with an average of three trials, while the class A player and
the beginner required four and six trials, respectively.

The most dramatic difference between the subjects, however, was
in the number of pieces correctly placed on the first trial. Figure 2.1
shows that in the middle-game positions, the Master was able to
place about sixteen pieces, while the class A player correctly recalled,
on average, eight pieces, and the beginner only four pieces. In the
end-game reconstructions the Master recalled, on average, eight
pieces, the class A player seven pieces, and the beginner four pieces.
Interestingly, the superiority of the Master over the other subjects

was not maintained beyond the first trial. On subsequent trials, when the subjects were able to see the position boards again, the Master usually added about four more pieces whereas the other subjects were able to add about five or six pieces on the second and subsequent trials.

The results from the reconstructions of meaningless, or random positions show that players of all levels of skill were lucky to recall three pieces accurately on the first trial, and things did not greatly improve in this condition on any of the subsequent trials.

One possible explanation for the Master's ability to recall twice as much as the class A player and four times as much as the beginner on the first trial for meaningful positions is that the Master has a very large (visual) short-term memory span. Perhaps skill in chess is correlated with superior short-term memory capacity. Chase and Simon were able to discount this explanation of the Master's performance because of the results from the reconstructions of meaningless, or random, positions. In this situation the results show that experts were no better at reconstructing positions than novices.

On the basis of these results, Chase and Simon hypothesized that in real-game situations, highly skilled players perceive *relations* between pieces, whereas duffers perceive little more than the positions of individual pieces on the board. De Groot has suggested that a Master's long-term memory contains a vast array of stored patterns. These patterns are memory representations of legitimate meaningful board positions that are categorized in terms of clusters of pieces attacking or defending each other. Perceived board positions could be recognized as matching stored memory representations.

Chase and Simon estimated that a chess Master has stored in memory 50,000 to 100,000 such patterns, or 'chunks' of information as they called them. If you think this sounds like a ridiculous claim, remember that the vocabulary of a university educated person is estimated to be about 50,000 to 100,000 words. Thus, just as an experienced reader is presumed to have word recognition units for thousands of letter patterns, or chunks (that is, words), the chess Master is presumed to have pattern recognition units for 'pawn chain', 'castled-king position' and many other chess positions. The difference between the pattern recognition abilities of the skilled and unskilled chess player would be like the difference between the word recognition abilities of university educated adults and the recognition of individual letters by primary school children. Besides knowing more individual words, the adult is likely to recognize whole chunks of commonly occurring words.

In order to discover exactly what these chunks of information might be, Chase and Simon devised a perception task. In this experiment, subjects were videotaped while they reconstructed positions on a board — as in the memory experiment — but this time the subjects were allowed to glance back at the original board position as often as they wished. The presumption was that, each time subjects glanced at the board, they would encode one meaningful pattern (reflecting one chunk stored in long-term memory). Chase and Simon analysed groups of pieces placed on the reconstruction board after each glance and found that the most frequently occurring patterns for the Master were (a) pawn chains, (b) castled-king positions, (c) clusters of pieces of the same colour, (d) attack, and (e) defence relations. The less skilled players also appeared to use some of the same chunks, but each chunk contained fewer pieces than the chunks of the Master.

In further experiments, Chase and Simon also demonstrated that, as well as knowing about relational patterns between chess pieces, chess Masters know stereotyped sequences of moves. In one experiment, a novice, an expert and a Master were required to memorize a twenty-five move game (actually fifty moves, as the moves of both players were counted as one move in the experiment). The Master required only ten minutes to learn the moves, while the class A player and the novice took half an hour and an hour and a half respectively. The Master made only four errors in learning the move sequence, the class A player made thirteen errors, and the novice made ninety-four errors.

In summary, Chase and Simon argued that the superior performance of a chess Master, by comparison with less able players, is a result of the Master's perception of patterns consisting of complex attack, defence and other relations between pieces on a chessboard during a game. These perceived patterns depend on the way a chess Master's knowledge is organized in long-term memory. Non-expert players, on the other hand, either have not yet acquired knowledge of meaningful configurations of pieces, or have not yet learned how to utilize this knowledge.

This research draws our attention to the importance of knowledge in skilled problem solving. Research on puzzle-like problems stressed general processes such as means-ends analysis. Research on chess suggests that processes like this may be only the first resort of unknowledgeable players. When we know nothing about a problem we have to work out from first principles a sequence of 'best' moves. But when we are faced with a problem we have experienced often before we can 'run off' patterns of already learnt responses. Since most of the 'problems' we encounter in real life are analogous to previous experience, we are already prepared with the necessary knowledge; although, as was demonstrated earlier, people do not always appreciate analogies or know how to apply solutions. However, in situation like chess, which has stereotyped sequences of moves, an expert can classify game situations in terms of known patterns of play, and is able to call on stored knowledge of how to deal with new situations that arise. (This is not to suggest that Grand Masters (or experts in any other field) never have to do any problem solving — that they've stored solutions to every possible problem with which they'll ever be confronted. The objective is to draw attention to the great importance of considerable, highly structured knowledge in expert problem solving.)

Computer programming

In the domain of computer programming, McKeithen, Reitman, Rueter and Hirtle (1981) asked groups of computer programmers of different levels of skill to recall computer programs that were presented briefly on a computer's visual display unit. Just as Chase and Simon presented both meaningful and non-meaningful chess positions, McKeithen *et al.* presented meaningful computer programs and programs in which lines of instructions had been randomly scrambled. They found that expert programmers were extraordinarily good at recalling meaningful programs. Novice programmers performed very poorly on this task, and intermediate-level programmers performed about halfway between the novices and experts. However, experts were no better than anyone else at recalling the scrambled programs.

McKeithen *et al.* argued that the performance of the experts was based on the organization of their knowledge in long-term memory. They tested the hypothesis by asking the different groups of subjects to memorize and recall lists of programming 'keywords' — elementary computer program instructions and concepts, such as 'string', 'real', 'bits', 'false', 'while', 'and', 'or' and 'do' — and analysed the order in which the keywords were recalled by the different groups. They found that experts organized the material for recall in a way that reflected meaningful programming relationships between the words (for example, 'while', 'do', 'for' and 'step') while novices organized the words according to natural language associations. For example, many novices would recall 'bits', 'of' and 'string' together, three words which when put together like that have an obvious meaning to most people but which make up a meaningless combination in terms of computer programming. McKeithen *et al.* argued that such recall orders reflected the unorganized nature of the novices' knowledge of programming.

In another experiment on novice and expert computer programmers, Adelson (1981) used a free recall task in order to uncover the underlying organization of knowledge of her subjects. Adelson presented her subjects with sixteen lines of code from the PPL programming language. The sixteen lines of code were taken from three real programs, but she presented the lines of code in scrambled order. All subjects were allowed to view the sixteen lines of code for twenty seconds, and were then given eight minutes to recall all they could. Each subject went through eight such trials, each time with twenty seconds viewing time and eight minutes recall time. Adelson showed that, as trials proceeded, experts started to group together the lines of code that 'belonged together' in the original three routines. In contrast, novice programmers grouped together lines of code that looked alike.

Adelson argued that experts used their knowledge of the various routines to organize the lines of program code into sensible groupings that belonged to particular routines. This research provides additional support for the hypothesis that experts have a hierarchy of knowledge about a domain which enables them to organize clusters of information into higher order structures, like chess games and computer programs. It is these functional information structures that give experts such a great advantage over novices in a wide range of tasks. In the terminology of schema theory it could be said that the experts have more highly organized *schemas*, which represent their knowledge structures about a particular domain.

Physics
The importance of problem schemas has been convincingly shown in a series of experiments conducted by Chi, Feltovich and Glaser (1981). In one of these experiments, Chi *et al.* asked PhD students (experts) and undergraduate students (novices) in physics to group twenty-four problems from a standard undergraduate physics textbook into categories, based on similarities in the way the problems should be solved. Interestingly, the experts took slightly (but not significantly) longer than the novices to sort the problems into categories, but both groups produced about eight or nine different problem categories altogether. The two groups did differ in terms of the problems they thought should be grouped together. The experts classified problems on the basis of fundamental laws of physics, such as Newton's first law. Novices, on the other hand, grouped problems on the basis of 'surface' features of the problems. For example, novices were likely to categorize two problems as members of the same class if the diagrams accompanying the problems both showed blocks on an inclined plane. In fact, the novices tended to call such problems 'inclined plane' problems. The experts, however, were able to distinguish between different types of problems that had surface similarities; rather, they grouped problems in terms of deep solution principles, such as 'Conservation of energy'. Chi *et al.* concluded that experts' problem-solving schemas contain knowledge that enables them to classify problems in terms of the solution principles that should be used to solve particular types of problems.

4.2 So, what is expertise?

In research into differences between novices and experts in other domains, such as medical diagnosis and architecture, the same pattern of results has emerged. One major difference between novices and experts is that experts can rely on memorized solutions to many problems in their domain (this is one of the reasons they are experts), while novices can seldom call on a very large store of answers to the problems with which they are confronted.

Memory for solutions to previously encountered problems is not the whole answer to the question of what it is to be expert in some domain, of course, because there are numerous problems with which any expert will be confronted for the first time. There are also differences in the strategies used by novices and experts to solve problems, even when the expert can't simply retrieve the solution from memory. Bhaskar and Simon (1977) have shown that experts work 'forwards' to find a problem solution, using the material presented in a problem statement to make inferences about information that will be needed to solve a problem. Novices, on the other hand, tend to work 'backwards' from the goal or use means-ends analysis for trying out and evaluating different operations. When experts are put into task situations with which they are unfamiliar, they too tend to fall back on means-ends analysis as a general problem-solving method.

A lot of recent research has shown that there are important differences between the way novices and experts *represent* a problem. Simon and Simon (1978) found evidence for such differences in their research on problem solving by a novice and an expert in physics. Their novice subject went straight to work on the problem after reading the problem statement, but the expert first worked on constructing a more concrete representation of the problem. More recently, Chi, Feltovich and Glaser (1981), in a mammoth study of the differences between novices and experts in solving physics problems, have shown that novices try to understand a problem by paying attention to the kinds of objects mentioned in the problem statement rather than relating the objects to deep, underlying principles as experts do.

Summary of Section 4

- Research in a number of different domains such as chess and computer programming indicates that skilled performance is based on highly organized domain-specific knowledge. Experts have a store of patterns representing commonly occurring configurations of information in the knowledge domain, and a store of solutions/operations to apply to them.

- One difference between novices and experts is the way they represent problems. Experts classify problems within their domain in terms of underlying principles and spend time reformulating problems during problem solving.
- Another difference is in terms of the strategies employed. Experts tend to work 'forwards' while novices tend to work 'backwards' from the goal, or use means-ends analysis in solving problems.
- The importance of problem-solving schemas in physics has been shown by Chi, Feltovich and Glaser, who found that novice physicists grouped problems according to surface features, while experts grouped them on the basis of fundamental laws of physics corresponding to the solution principles that should be used.

5   Learning

We have seen how experts differ from novices, but a central question that has not yet been addressed is: how do people get to be experts as a result of practice at solving problems in a particular domain? In other words, what are the mechanisms underlying the transition from being a novice in, say, chess, to becoming an expert? Modelling human learning is one of the central problems in psychology and one that has attracted the interest of many psychologists working with computer models. Learning and memory are, of course, closely related mechanisms. It is often through learning, deliberate or incidental, that the contents of long-term memory are established and modified.

5.1   Declarative and procedural knowledge

As a mundane example of an expert performance, consider the duties of the cabin staff on an aeroplane. Cabin staff have to deal with situations as varied as distributing meals within a set amount of time, caring for sick passengers (anything from drunkenness to contagious diseases), decompression, emergency landings, and fires.

Each of these tasks is composed of a number of activities that have to be coordinated and swiftly executed. For instance, if a member of the cabin staff notices smoke coming from an oven in the galley, he or she should switch off the oven, pull the circuit breaker, isolate the area (remove anything that is combustible, including people), get the fire extinguisher, and get someone (not a passenger) to inform the flight deck. He or she *should not* open the oven door, and should use the fire extinguisher only if flames appear. Efficient performance depends on knowing how to switch off the oven; knowing where the nearest fire extinguisher is, how to unfasten it from its fitting, and how to use it if necessary; and knowing how to inform other members of the staff without terrifying the passengers.

When people are trained to perform such activities, they generally start out by memorizing what it is they have to do (see if you can remember what should be done if you see smoke coming from an oven). This type of knowledge is termed *declarative knowledge* because it consists of declarative statements (for example, the statement that a fire extinguisher is used to put out fires). The important point to grasp is that declarative knowledge is at the level of *verbal knowledge*; that is, the kind of knowledge you get from books, instructions, or being told what to do.

In order to achieve skilled performance you need to be able to translate declarative knowledge into actions. A new form of representation, known as *procedural knowledge*, must be established. A good example is learning to drive a car: there is the world of difference between knowing that you need to change gears, and being able to do so. In the initial stages of learning from instructions, people often forget one or another of the components. With practice, skilled performance becomes better integrated, and speeds up considerably. In other words, the expert learns to respond to whole patterns rather than to individual components of a situation. (The driver 'changes down to third' instead of 'moving the gear lever from the bottom right position to the top right'.)

*ACT**

Section 4 presented evidence from domains such as chess, physics and computer programming which indicates that expert problem solving depends to a great extent on already stored domain-specific knowledge. In this section I want to describe a theory of learning called ACT* (ACT star) which has been developed by John Anderson and implemented in computer models. The theory attempts to account for the full range of cognitive functioning, from pattern recognition through to problem solving, and has in fact undergone a number of reformulations over the years. Because of the wide range of ACT*'s application, it is not possible to describe the theory here in any great detail. (There is a very readable, and highly recommended, account of Anderson's theory in his book *The Architecture of Cognition* (1983). A briefer account can be found in Cohen, Kiss and Le Voi, *Memory: Current Issues* (1993).)

In Anderson's theory, long-term memory contains both declarative and procedural knowledge. Declarative knowledge is represented in a kind of semantic network, while procedural knowledge is represented in the form of a production system. Briefly, a production system consists of sets of rules of the form 'IF <condition> and <condition> ... THEN <action>'. A simple example would be 'IF you are driving towards a junction and the traffic light is red THEN prepare to stop'. Production systems force researchers to be quite specific about the organization of information in long-term memory and the way in which that information is accessed and used, but if a production system is to model learning, then new productions must somehow be added to the system's production (or procedural) memory. This has led Anderson and others to the idea that some kinds of human learning may also consist of the piecemeal addition of new productions for performing actions in response to certain conditions.

In ACT*, Anderson claims that people progress through three successive stages of learning in acquiring cognitive skills.

1 The first stage of learning involves the accumulation of domain-relevant facts which are incorporated into the system's declarative network structure. In learning chess, for example, a novice would acquire a number of facts or rules governing the direction of moves possible for each chess piece, such as: 'a bishop can be moved along diagonals', or 'a knight can be moved forward (sideways, backward) two squares and over one square'. Pre-existing general problem-solving processes (for example, working backwards) would then employ these facts in solving problems. A major advantage of declarative knowledge is that it is general in the sense that there is no commitment to its use in some specific manner, such as would be the case if the knowledge were represented procedurally. The main drawback of declarative knowledge is that before it can be used it must be retrieved and kept active in working memory. In ACT*, the slow pace and tentative nature of problem solving during this stage of learning are attributed to the need to activate and retrieve declarative knowledge from long-term memory (for example, rules about the direction in which a knight may be moved). A chess player operating at this level takes a long time to figure out a move. Also, loss of information from working memory is seen as a major source of errors during problem solving.

2 With experience, however, Anderson claims that declarative knowledge becomes proceduralized. In this second, *transitional stage* of learning, to use the terminology of production systems, new productions are created from the declarative knowledge acquired during the first stage of learning. The mechanism underlying the transition between the first two stages is called *proceduralization*. Proceduralization is a process that transforms declarative information in long-term memory into procedures for actions. The outcome of proceduralization is that declarative knowledge becomes embedded

in procedures, and the result of the process is that conscious retrieval of information from declarative memory becomes unnecessary.
As an example from chess again, after some experience, moving a
knight from its current position on the board to another position will
become automatic — there is no need consciously to retrieve the
declarative knowledge that 'a knight can be moved forward (sideways,
backward) two squares and over one square'. The learner comes to
'see' moves directly (because the knowledge becomes embedded in
productions which are automatically activated). Eliminating the need
for conscious search and retrieval of declarative information from
long-term memory not only has the effect of speeding up performance but also reduces the load on working memory and so reduces
the likelihood of errors.

3 In the final stage of learning in ACT*, the *procedural stage*, the
productions that have been acquired are tuned, or smoothed out. In
essence, during this stage the learner acquires considerable knowledge about the *specific conditions* in which a production should fire.
In the chess example, the learner comes to recognize that moving
the knight should be preceded by a consideration of the consequences
of making the move (an opposing piece might be in a position to
capture the knight). In this stage another process called *generalization*
occurs in which the learner also generalizes what has been learned
(e.g. sacrificing a piece in order to capture a piece of greater value
or for strategic advantage is a good thing), and the application of
knowledge speeds up considerably due to a *strengthening* process.
The strength of each production is increased each time it is used.
Productions that are used infrequently are weakened through an
automatic strength reduction process. As the chess player becomes
more expert, good moves are strengthened and poor moves drop
out.

   In ACT*, speed-up in performance is also partly attributed to a
mechanism called *composition*, which is a process that combines two
components of a skill into a larger ('macro') component. In composition, a new production is constructed from a pair of already-
existing productions which are related to the same goal, and which
occur reliably in succession during problem solving. In chess, for
example, a sequence of stereotyped moves would be combined into
a single production, generally used in openings and sometimes in
end-games.

SAQ 15
Describe how proceduralization, strengthening, and composition might affect the
performance of air cabin staff coping with a fire.

Anderson and his various collaborators have constructed a number of computer programs to test the assumptions embodied in ACT* and have compared the performance of the programs with human performance in a number of different learning environments. Examples are computer programming (Anderson, Farrell and Sauers, 1984; Pirolli and Anderson, 1985), geometry (Anderson, Greeno, Kline and Neves, 1981), and language acquisition (Anderson, 1983). The models provide quite detailed accounts of problem solving and learning in all of the domains that have been studied. In particular, they show how a learning system which starts off with only a number of domain-related facts stored in declarative long-term memory, plus a number of pre-existing general problem-solving procedures (such as procedures for solving problems by analogy to worked out examples presented in instructional material), can acquire new procedures that are responsive to the kind of situations that occur in the domain of learning. The simulations demonstrate that skill acquisition can be modelled by the addition and modification of production rules. Mechanisms such as proceduralization and composition transform a system that initially works backwards (novice strategy) into one that works forwards (like experts).

The main problem with the simulations is that they often perform better than the human subjects whose behaviour they are meant to model. As an example, Anderson (1982) describes a simulation of the behaviour of high-school students solving two-column problems in geometry. The 'simulation' solved these problems but not all the students did. In fact, simulations based on ACT* often seem to provide us with models of the idealized problem solving and learning of 'good' students, rather than of the average student who experiences considerable difficulty in solving problems, and in learning to derive procedures from declarative instructions.

Summary of Section 5

- ACT* models learning in terms of adding and altering productions in long-term production memory.
- In ACT*, knowledge is represented in both declarative and procedural form. In the initial stage of skill acquisition, knowledge is represented as a number of facts in propositional network structures in long-term memory. The second stage of learning involves the transformation of declarative knowledge into procedures for applying knowledge directly. During the final stage of learning, procedural knowledge is refined by processes such as composition, generalization and strengthening.

- Composition is a process that constructs 'macro-operators' by combining a pair of productions that are related to the same goal, and that reliably follow one another in a problem-solving task.
- The generalization process makes alterations to the condition part of similar productions so that the production can apply in other similar, but novel conditions.
- Each time a production rule is applied its strength is automatically increased. Production rules that apply infrequently gradually lose strength through an automatic strength decrement process.

6   Conclusions

We know a lot more today about analogical problem solving than we knew ten years ago. As described in Part I, we know that problem-solving strategies can be transferred between well-defined problem isomorphs if the conditions are right. The more recent research described in Part I attempts to detail the strategies used to solve these well-defined problems and how features of the task environment play a major role in determining the strategies.

Today we know that learning can also be transferred between ill-defined, distantly related problems, but the transfer is not automatic. People need experience with a number of examples of a particular type of problem in order to be able to abstract the common elements, to develop a problem schema, before they can automatically bring their knowledge to bear on subsequent problems. Processes involved in mapping analogs on to one another and in abstracting a generalized schema from a number of specific problem-solving instances, and the ways in which analogical problem solving and other problem-solving processes interact, are poorly understood.

On the plus side, computer simulation models of analogical problem-solving have begun to appear. Over the next few years we can expect improvements in such models — improvements here meaning becoming better able to model human performance — once the prototypes have been built and their designers can afford to have more regard for human performance data. At the same time, the computer models will suggest testable hypotheses about processes of interest. Improved models of memory organization and retrieval processes would have a major impact on such studies.

Part III
The Experimental Analysis of Analogical Reasoning

Contents

1   Introduction

Everywhere we've looked in this book we've found *individual differences* in problem-solving behaviour, although we haven't yet discussed research in this light. For example, in research on the Missionaries and Cannibals/Jealous Husbands problems (see Part I, Section 4.1) we have seen that most people failed to transfer experience from one version of the problem to another (either the MC problem followed by the JH problem or vice versa) unless they were given a hint that the two problems were related, and then only if the second problem was simpler than the first (i.e. the JH problem followed by the MC problem). Nevertheless, the fact is that although most people failed to benefit from prior experience without a hint, *some* did.

Again, when Gick and Holyoak presented the fortress/radiation problems (see Part II, Section 1.3, Techniques Box C), approximately 20 per cent of their subjects solved the radiation problem because they noticed the relationship between it and the prior fortress problem without being given a hint that they were related. Why? And why did the other 80 per cent fail to notice the similarity? When another group of subjects were given a hint to use the earlier problem, 92 per cent of them were able to come up with the required solution (which still leaves 8 per cent who were unable to benefit from the hint). Part III explores some answers to the problem posed by individual differences in problem solving.

We also discussed novice/expert differences, and described some of the learning mechanisms involved in transiting from being a novice to being an expert, as embodied in the ACT* model of learning. But we didn't tackle questions such as, 'Why don't *all* novices become experts?', or, 'Why, given a classroom full of students learning the same new subject matter, do some students consistently achieve As for their work, some Cs, and others fail?' Almost invariably, 'average' students would like to achieve As, and students who consistently fail would like to start passing their courses. The question we ask in Part III is, 'Can anything be done to help people achieve such commendable goals?'

A common view of the reason why people differ in what they manage to achieve in academic or problem-solving situations (and, indeed, other situations, including social situations) is that some people, for one reason or another, just happen to be smarter than others.

In common parlance, some people have higher IQs, and the higher the IQ the quicker or more likely a person is to learn. In fact, it has been known for some time that IQ is a good predictor of how well a person will perform in *academic situations* (but, *nota bene*, not in real-life situations outside the classroom); the higher the IQ, the more likely it is that a person will be successful in such situations. It is implicit in this view of intelligence that there are some ideas that only the highly intelligent can readily grasp, that there are some procedures that you can't acquire unless you're 'really smart', that 'creativity' is a special kind of thinking usually reserved to people with really high IQs, and so on. It is also thought by some that a person's intelligence is more or less fixed for life, that intelligence is an inbuilt, unalterable property of the brain. This, of course, would be bad news for people of 'average' or 'below average' intelligence who would like to improve themselves if only there were some way to do it.

But this is not a view that necessarily has to be accepted at this point in our understanding of the nature of intelligence. Consider some research carried out by Schoenfeld (1979), who hypothesized that learning might be made more efficient if students were taught domain-specific strategies. In Schoenfeld's experiment, two groups of students spent twenty hours solving mathematics problems. Both groups performed about equally well on a pre-experimental test that involved solving a small number of mathematics problems. An experimental group was then presented with a list of useful problem-solving strategies, and was given practice at applying the strategies on twenty exercise problems. The control group was also asked to solve the exercise problems, but was not given instruction in the use of special strategies. In a post-experimental test, the experimental subjects were able to solve approximately three times as many problems as they had solved in the pre-experimental test. The control subjects showed no improvement at all on the post-experimental problems.

That research has interesting implications. Maybe people who are good at solving problems (including problems given on intelligence tests, the tasks that determine a person's IQ) have somehow *learned* good strategies for acquiring and organizing information and for solving different types of problems. It may be that people who are not so good at solving problems just haven't acquired optimal strategies. Such hypotheses lead one to think that if one knew what the optimal strategies were, and if one found that less successful solvers showed signs of having acquired poorer strategies, then they could be taught the more useful strategies. Once these better strategies had been acquired, a person's performance (including performance on intelligence tests) should improve. The nice thing, I believe, about information-processing psychology is that this is the kind of thinking that motivates the research of its adherents.

In a restricted sense, Part III is about 'the nature of intelligence', but only in a very restricted sense. It's about the nature of intelligence because it describes recent attempts by cognitive psychologists, particularly those working within the information-processing paradigm, to address questions of what constitutes intelligence and to relate what they find to problems of learning in the classroom. We're not going to be able to discuss the many other important and interesting views of the nature of intelligence that have emerged in the past couple of decades; nor will we be concerned with some of the enduring questions that have exercised the minds and laboratories of psychologists who are interested in intelligence, such as the question of the contribution of genes to the limits of a person's intelligence, whether there are racial differences in intelligence, or whether tests that are designed without a concern for the social or motivational aspects of intelligence are measuring real intelligence in people. These and other issues, however, are discussed in *Introduction to Psychology*, vol. 1 (Roth, 1990), which is recommended as an introduction to these and other issues in intelligence research.

Summary of Section 1

- People differ in their ability to use prior experience in solving current problems. Some people seem to be able to use prior experience spontaneously, whilst others seem unable to use such experience even when given a hint that such prior experience would be useful in a new problem situation.
- IQ has long been known to be a good predictor of what people will achieve in academic situations (i.e. classrooms in schools and colleges). A person's IQ is not, however, a good predictor of what someone can or will achieve in the world outside of the classroom.
- Information-processing psychologists have been interested in improving the performance of students on cognitive tasks regardless of their measured IQ. A basic premise of their approach is that good students have acquired optimal strategies for solving problems and learning, and that these strategies, once they have been catalogued, can be taught to students who have not done so well or who have failed in the past.
- Schoenfeld has demonstrated that when students are taught domain-specific problem-solving strategies they show massive improvement over students who are not provided with such instruction.

2   *Psychometric and componential analyses of intelligence*

In this section I shall outline and contrast the psychometric (Section 2.1) and the componential (Section 2.2) approaches to understanding intelligence. This introduction will serve as a useful background for the fuller discussion of the componential analysis approach which will occupy the rest of the book from Section 4 onwards.

2.1   Psychometrics

The unit of analysis with which *psychometricians* (a term used for people who devise intelligence and personality tests) are concerned is called the *factor*. A factor is a mathematical concept derived from statistical analyses of multiple correlations among batteries of tests. The factors that are discovered are given 'meaningful' labels, such as *verbal ability*, or the *verbal factor*. This factor would be said to account for a person's performance on a group of tests such as 'vocabulary' or 'reading comprehension'. Experts still argue about the number of factors that need to be postulated in order to account for intelligence, ranging between one (Spearman, 1923) and one hundred and fifty (Guilford, 1967). Between these two extremes, most experts now think there are about a dozen factors that should be included in any definition of what it is that comprises intelligence, including *mathematical ability, verbal comprehension, deduction, induction, memory span* and *spatial visualization*. One of the major disputes between psychometricians has been over whether there is a *general factor* (the single factor postulated by Spearman) of intelligence. The issue is whether there is such a thing as general intelligence that impacts on all intellectual tasks, as opposed to *specific abilities* which different people either do or do not have. In essence, the question is whether people who are good lawyers would have been good scientists or good engineers or good businessmen, if they had chosen one of these other occupations, just because they have a fairly high level of general mental ability. The alternative view, of course, would be that good doctors are just that because they have some particular ability or group of abilities that are required to make good doctors. Some cognitive psychologists believe that general problem-solving mechanisms, such as means-ends analysis and analogy, underlie general intelligence, while domain-specific problem-solving procedures comprise the specific abilities measured by IQ tests.

2.2   Componential analysis

Psychometricians have only been able to measure abilities (e.g. verbal ability, spatial ability, induction, number ability, etc.) and to say how they relate to each other, thus providing global 'maps' of cognitive functions. Such maps are useful to psychologists, because they indicate which types of ability to analyse. However, psychometric analyses do not tell us anything about the actual mental processes that underlie abilities such as divergent thinking or number ability (i.e. they tell us what the different abilities are, but not how they work). Cognitive psychologists have moved into the field of intelligence in order to try to provide a deeper and more specific understanding of the processes involved in intelligence. Knowing that people are good at maths because they achieve high scores on tests of number ability isn't the most helpful statement that might be made about the relationship between intelligence and achievement. In fact, it could equally be argued that the opposite holds true — people achieve high scores on tests of number ability if they have attained a high degree of skill at maths. We don't want to be left in the unhelpful position of having to tell people who want to be better mathemeticians that they need to do better on the part of intelligence tests that measures number ability.

It was this lack of understanding of the actual cognitive processes underlying skilled performance that led to some dissatisfaction with the psychometric approach, and posed a challenge to cognitive psychologists to provide explanatory mechanisms for factors such as verbal ability. Cognitive psychologists attempt to explain reasoning in terms of the way people represent or understand a particular problem, the load imposed on a restricted WM capacity, retrieval of information from LTM, and so on.

In componential analysis, investigators use tasks which are found on standard intelligence tests as the focus of research. The idea is to understand how good and poor performances can be related to detailed information-processing models, and to see how what is learned can be related to (and suggest modifications in) classroom learning situations. Pellegrino and Glaser (1982) stated it this way:

> The global objective is to contribute to an understanding of the ways in which individuals differ in abilities for learning. In the long run, our goal will be achieved if we can couch abilities to learn in terms of the concepts of modern cognitive theory, and then develop procedures for identifying school-related capabilities based upon these interpretations ... our initial step is to accept the robust correlational fact of a relationship between certain abilities measured by test tasks and school achievement. We then identify classes of test tasks that have consistently appeared on scholastic aptitude tests and use current techniques of task analysis to understand the nature of the performance elicited by these tasks. A logical next step would be to relate the aptitude processes to similar task analytic work being pursued in school subject matter areas, e.g. beginning reading, text comprehension, elementary arithmetic, science problem solving, etc. Such an approach should begin to explain the predictive validity of the skills of learning measured by scholastic aptitude tests, and the reasons for limitations in validity, and may suggest how instruction could improve the intellectual performances involved. (pp. 273–4)

Pellegrino and Glaser, in the above quotation, call for:

(a) concentration of research effort on some ability that is measured

by intelligence tests, one that is known to predict future performance in another place (i.e. the classroom), and then
(b) the use of modern task analysis techniques to understand performance on a whole class of tasks that are used to measure that particular ability.

The central ability we shall be looking at is inductive ability (which will
be defined with examples in Section 3). Inductive ability has traditionally been measured by a number of different tasks, including series
completion problems (e.g. 1, 3, 7, 13 ... What number comes next?),
classification problems (e.g. Which continuation option best fits in with
the first three terms of the analogy? Zebra, Giraffe, Lion, (a) Dog
(b) Cat, (c) Parrot, (d) Deer), and analogies (e.g. Dog is to Cat as
Puppy is to What?). Inductive ability is interesting to us because it has
long been known to psychometricians and educators to be a good
predictor of scholastic achievement (i.e. people who score high on
this ability on intelligence tests generally tend to do well in academic
learning situations, while those who achieve low scores tend to do
poorly in those same situations).

Summary of Section 2

- Psychometrics is the name for the study and measurement of human
  intelligence (and personality, but that is not a concern of ours here).
  Theoretical psychometrics is concerned with the identification of intellectual abilities and the way they relate one to another.
- A major dispute in intelligence research concerns whether there is
  such a thing as general intelligence (or general intelligence plus some
  number of specific abilities), or whether the concept of general intelligence should be dropped in favour of a conception of intelligence as a number of specific abilities.
- Dissatisfaction with the psychometric approach arose from its dis-
  regard for the processes underlying intelligence. Cognitive psychologists set out to provide accounts of intelligence in terms of the
  component processes involved in reasoning and problem solving.
- Cognitive psychologists are also interested in training intelligence —
  or problem solving or reasoning abilities — in order to help people
  improve their performance in classroom situations.
- Inductive ability is a good predictor of academic achievement and as
  such has become a focus for research in cognitive psychology.

3   *Induction*

Imagine some being from outer space watching a set of traffic lights here on earth, and observing the flow of traffic. After an hour of attending to events, our visitor might form rules like 'Whenever a traffic light is red, cars stop', and 'When the light is green, cars move'. This is *induction*: a process of hypothesizing a general rule that represents common features of a set of specific objects or events.

However, induction is a risky kind of reasoning, because it is not always possible to observe all possible objects or events, so it is not certain that the rule will always hold. In the current example, some people drive across red lights and some people stall their cars when the light changes from red to green. Inductive rules are generally, but not always, right.

Induction can be regarded as the opposite of deduction. In induction, we go from the specific (observing particular cars stopping at traffic lights) to a general rule ('If the light is red, stop'). In deduction, we go in the other direction, using general knowledge to solve specific problems. Thus, when we drive towards a green light we assume that the driver of the car in front of us will keep going at a green light rather than suddenly slamming on the brakes. We can say that induction is the name for some set of cognitive processes that enables us to abstract rules from experience. Similarly, deduction is the set of processes used to apply the rules we have acquired (e.g. deriving specific knowledge such as 'Socrates is mortal' from the two bits of knowledge 'Socrates is a man' and 'All men are mortal'). Thus, induction is associated with learning processes, whereas deduction is associated with the application of our knowledge.

In the following discussion we shall be exclusively concerned with *analogical reasoning* as a task that measures a person's inductive ability. One good reason for this is that we have already discussed *analogical problem solving research* in Part II. Traditionally, these two research strands have been investigated separately, with little cross-talk between them. The major difference between the two traditions has been that in analogical problem solving research experimental tasks have more of a real-world flavour (e.g. the fortress/radiation problems investigated by Gick and Holyoak or the mathematics problems investigated by Reed and his collaborators, described in Part II). They are also larger scale, more open-ended problems than analogical reasoning tasks, which are highly structured and confined, for the most part, to use as intelligence tests.

Another reason for limiting our discussion to analogies is that theoreticians in psychometrics (Spearman; Burt; Raven; Miller), psychology (Tyler; Glaser; Sternberg; Whiteley), and artificial intelligence

(Carbonell; Schank) have claimed that analogical reasoning is a central thought process. Spearman in fact regarded the proportional analogy (described in Section 3.1 below) as the paradigmatic case of induction, 'the prototype of intelligent thought' (quoted in Bejar, Chaffin, and Embretson, 1991).

A final reason for concentrating on analogical reasoning is that this type of task has been more thoroughly researched by more people than any other task measuring inductive ability. The componential analysis of analogical reasoning involves an attempt at a detailed understanding of analogical reasoning in terms of elementary information processes. A major goal is to find out what distinguishes between good and poor solvers on a particular task. Perhaps people with different abilities use different strategies (different ways of organizing the elementary processes). Another goal would be to try to alter the strategies of people who are not so good at analogical reasoning in the light of what is learnt about how good reasoners do it.

By the end of Part III you should have a fair grasp of what is known about analogical reasoning processes; indeed, I hope that you will be able to improve your own performance on such tasks if you practise what you learn here. You should also understand the strengths and limitations of componential analysis, and see how componential and psychometric approaches are potentially mutually complementary rather than conflicting approaches to understanding intelligence.

3.1   *Proportional analogies*

A proportional analogy is an analogy of the form A:B::C:D (A is to B as C is to D). An analogy problem is one where one of the terms is left blank and has to be supplied by the solver. Such problems may appear in a number of different formats. An example of an analogy problem in *forced-choice format* (i.e. A:B::C: (a) D1 (b) D2) is:

Letter:Word::Sentence: (a) Chapter (b) Paragraph.

Here the solver must choose the best completion term from those on offer. The number of completion alternatives presented in forced-choice analogies generally ranges from two to five.

Analogies may also be presented in *production format* (i.e. A:B::C:?), for example:

Wide:Narrow::Thick: ?.

Such problems are said to be in production format because solvers are left to complete the analogy by *producing from their own knowledge* the last term, or solution, to the problem.

There is also a *true-false format* (i.e. A:B::C:D — True False), as in the example:

Bicycle:Handlebars::Automobile:Steering-wheel   True False.

In this format, of course, the solver is given an analogy and asked to indicate whether it is true or false.

We refer to the different parts of such analogy problems as the *terms* of the analogy — the A term ('Bicycle' in the last example above), the B term ('Handlebars'), the C term ('Automobile'), and the D term ('Steering-wheel'). We also speak of the *domain* of the analogy (the A:B terms together — 'Bicycle:Handlebars') and the *range* of the analogy (the C:D terms — 'Automobile:Steering-wheel'). Finally, the first three terms (A:B::C) together are referred to as the *stem* of the analogy. In such cases, the final term (D) is referred to as the *completion term*, or *solution term*.

SAQ 16
1 In the analogy

Simon:Information Processing::Skinner: ?

what are: (a) the domain of the analogy, (b) the range, (c) the stem, and (d) the completion term?
2 What is the answer?

Solving an analogy, in general terms, involves finding a *relation* between the C and D terms of the analogy that matches (as closely as possible) the relation between the A and B terms. In fact, the very essence of analogical reasoning is finding a *second order relation* that acts as a link between the *first order relations* holding between the domain and range of the analogy — a relation that logically subsumes the first order relations. For example, in the analogy

Bicycle:Handlebars::Automobile:Steering-wheel

the first order relation between 'Bicycle' and 'Handlebars' can be thought of as 'steered by'. The first order relation between 'Automobile' and 'Steering-wheel' is also 'steered by'. So the second order relation would be something like 'method of steering' (see Figure 3.1 overleaf).

However, if there were no second order relation linking the domain and range of an analogy, it would be a false analogy. Consider this problem:

Robin:Worm::Shark:Dangerous   True False.

The first order relation between 'Robin' and 'Worm' would be something like 'eats'. The first order relation between 'Shark' and

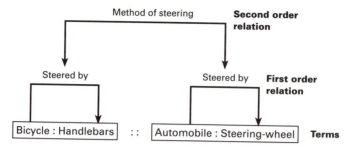

Figure 3.1

'Dangerous' would be something like 'has the property of being' or 'should be regarded as'. In this example, there is no second order relation we can think of that would provide a bridge between the first order relations, so it's a false analogy. We'd be more likely to accept the analogy if it had been either

   Robin:Harmless::Shark:Dangerous True False

or

   Robin:Worms::Shark:Fish True False.

SAQ 17

1 Below are a number of analogies for you to solve. The first three are in forced-choice format. The last problem is in production format:
 (a) Corporal:Beat::Capital: (a) Stun (b) Maim (c) Kill (d) Shock
 (b) Noon:Eve::12–21 (a) 6–00 (b) 18–30 (c) 10–01 (d) 4–00
 (c) Cowardly:Yellow::Gloomy: (a) Blue (b) Red (c) Ochre (d) White
 (d) Einstein:Relativity::Darwin: ?
2 Go back through the problems and (a) list the first order relation between the domain and range of each problem, and (b) list the second order relation for each problem.

3.2   Geometric analogies

Geometric analogies are another type of proportional analogy frequently found on intelligence tests. The structure, as shown in Figure 3.2, is the same as for verbal analogies. Each figure consists of a number of *elements* (in this case circles, triangles, squares, ovals and crosses) which differ along certain *dimensions* (e.g. position and size). The elements of the A term, in the Figure 3.2 analogy, are a large open circle, a triangle, and a small dark circle. The relations among the elements are (a) the triangle is centrally placed within the large open circle, and (b) the small dark circle is centrally placed below the large open circle. The B term has all the same elements as the A term but the relations have changed. In effect, the triangle and the small black circle have changed places: the triangle has been removed from the large open circle and placed centrally below it and the small dark circle has been moved so that it is centrally placed within the large open circle. In order to solve the problem the solver needs to analyse the C term to determine the elements and their position and then to apply the same *transformations* that had been discovered in the analysis of the differences between the A and B terms. An interesting feature of geometric analogies is that more or less complex stimuli can be generated simply by manipulating the number of elements, dimensions, and transformation rules between the different terms of a problem. Such problems are considerably more 'culture free' than the verbal analogies described in Section 3.1, where solution often depends on acquired knowledge, such as what lawyers and doctors do. When it comes to modelling cognitive processes in solving analogies, the ability to measure and manipulate complexity is an important consideration, as we shall see in later discussions of both geometric and verbal analogies.

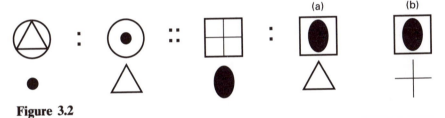

Figure 3.2

Activity 11
For each of the problems presented in Figure 3.3, list:
1 The number of elements.
2 The dimensions on which elements differ.
3 The transformational rule between the A and B terms.

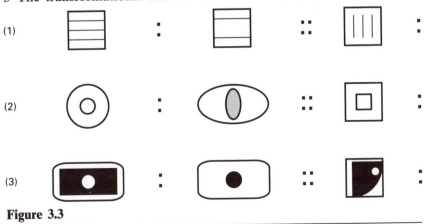

Figure 3.3

3.3   People-piece analogies

People-piece analogies consist of line drawings of people, as shown in Figure 3.4. Here, the dimensions of difference are size (large, small), shape (male-like, female-like), and shading (dark, light). As with geometric analogies, it is easy to manipulate the complexity of such problems by adding elements and transformations. People-piece analogies are an example of a type of analogy problem used by Robert Sternberg (whose work is discussed in the next two sections) in his extensive research on analogical reasoning.

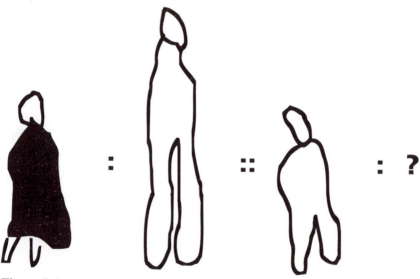

Figure 3.4

The appropriate completion for the problem shown in Figure 3.4 would be a tall woman in a black dress, since the transformation between the A and B terms involved going from a short woman in a black dress to a tall man in plain clothing (i.e. transformation one: change of sex; transformation two: colour change; transformation three: change of size).

Summary of Section 3

- Induction can be defined as a process of hypothesizing a general rule that represents common features of a set of specific objects or events.
- Analogical reasoning has been widely researched by cognitive psychologists as a prototypical example of inductive reasoning.
- Proportional analogies are analogies of the form A is to B as C is to What? These problems are presented in a number of different formats, including forced-choice, production, and true-false.

- The first two terms of a proportional analogy are referred to as the domain of the analogy; the final two terms are referred to as the range of the analogy. The first three terms together are called the stem of the analogy, while the last term by itself is called the completion or solution term.
- Analogy solution involves finding a relation between the terms in the range of the analogy that matches the relation between the terms in the domain of the analogy. The relations linking terms in both the domain and range of an analogy are called first order relations. The relation that links the first order relations is called a second order relation. The first order relations often are similar to one another rather than a direct match, so finding a second order relation that links them might involve considerable reasoning.

4   Componential analysis of analogical reasoning

The first problem confronting anyone who wants to give a detailed account of some cognitive performance is to identify the different cognitive processes involved in the task. Componential analysis of analogy problems works by breaking the problem down into its component parts and analysing the process(es) applied to each component. This can be done by a kind of 'armchair analysis' of the kinds of processes that might be involved. For analogy problems, one might argue for processes like perception, language understanding and storage of information in WM. These processes are required when a person is confronted with each single term of an analogy, such as 'Green'. The ability to discover relations between different terms of the analogy might be regarded as another process. Thus, given the first two terms of an analogy such as 'Green:Go', it is reasonable to argue that a solver needs to infer a relation such as 'means' or 'indicates' or 'signifies' between green and go in the context of driving on the roads (i.e. 'green means go'; 'green indicates go'; 'green signifies go', or whatever). In Figure 3.5, the two processes are indicated as (1) *encoding* (a general

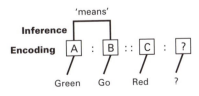

Figure 3.5

111

term to cover perception, retrieval of information from LTM and storage of (at least some of) that information in WM), and (2) *inference*, whereby the relation between the first two terms of the analogy is inferred.

Activity 12

Solve the following analogy — Lawyer : Client :: Doctor: (a) Hospital (b) Patient — but at the same time try to write notes on the processes you think you yourself bring into play during each step of the solution. This is an important activity, as it gives you a chance to try to identify and name processes that actually occur inside your head while you work on the problem and hence some feeling for the difficulty of performing such analyses.

Hint: Analogy solution involves fast processes below the level of conscious awareness. In order to organize your analysis it might be helpful to break the task down into subtasks, and consider each subtask in turn. For instance, the complete task given in this Activity can be broken down in terms of separate and combined parts of the task, which allows you to think about what you are doing when presented with, say, the A term of the analogy, or the terms in the domain of the analogy, and so forth, e.g.:

A
A:B
A:B::C
A:B::C: (a) D1, (b) D2

In other words, try to think about what comes into your head when you see 'Lawyer'; then 'Lawyer:Client'; then 'Lawyer:Client::Doctor'; then 'Lawyer:Client::Doctor:Hospital'; and finally 'Lawyer:Client:: Doctor:Patient'. You might also find it a help to use the diagram in Figure 3.6, which already indicates encoding and inference as two possible processes. You might want to draw other connecting lines between the different terms of the analogy to indicate where you think different processes come into play, and then give names to the different connecting links.

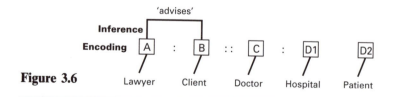

Figure 3.6

By now, you should have some sort of informed awareness of what processes go on when you solve a verbal analogy.

4.1   Sternberg's theory

The analysis in this section is based on a theory of analogical reasoning proposed by Sternberg (1977). Sternberg's task in identifying component processes was a lot easier than the task I set you in the last Activity, because he had an earlier process model (Spearman, 1923) which he was able to use as a framework for thinking about the analysis. In Spearman's model, three important processes had been outlined (see Figure 3.7): the *apprehension of experience*, the *eduction of relations*, and the *eduction of correlates*. In the simplest terms, apprehension of experience is Spearman's name for the process we have described as encoding; eduction of relations is the search for a relation between the first two terms of the analogy, or what we have called inference; and the eduction of correlates is the process whereby the relation between the A and B terms is automatically applied to the C term immediately the C term has been encoded (a process that Sternberg would call application, described below). Spearman has been credited with introducing the first information-processing model of analogy solution with the three principles outlined above (Sternberg, 1977), but unfortunately Spearman never tested and elaborated his model, mainly because the experimental techniques needed to test such models were not available in Spearman's time.

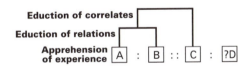

Figure 3.7   Spearman's process model of analogical reasoning

So part of what Sternberg has done has been to update the terminology of Spearman's model to bring it in line with modern cognitive concepts. Sternberg has also elaborated Spearman's model, in that he has (1) unpacked some of the processes in the older theory into subprocesses, and (2) suggested other processes as belonging in the solution sequence. In all, Sternberg claims that six components can account for all analogical reasoning:

1 Encoding   4 Application
2 Inference   5 Justification
3 Mapping   6 Response.

The rest of Section 4.1 will describe the details of this model by showing what is involved in each component as each term or sequence of terms of the analogy is presented or seen by the solver. Section 4.2 will describe different possible strategies, all of them involving the same six components, that solvers might use in solving analogy problems. In Section 4.3, we shall consider the research that has been conducted to find out which of these different strategies best describes human performance. We shall also consider, in Sections 4.3 and 4.4, differences between good and poor solvers with respect to these different models. We shall discuss objections to (and confirmations of) Sternberg's methods and conclusions and consider other models that have been proposed.

Stage 1: Encoding
When presented with the first term of an analogy — 'Lawyer', in the example in Activity 12 — you have to *encode* the stimulus: perceive it, retrieve information relating to it from LTM, and store some of this information in working memory (WM). We assume that encoding is called into play for all of the terms of the analogy as they are seen. Figure 3.8 shows the encoding process for the A term, with the yet unseen other terms of this particular problem shown as black squares. For the sake of (simplifying) argument, we assume that when 'Lawyer' is seen, the information that 'Lawyer is a licensed professional who provides legal advice' is retrieved from LTM and stored in WM for the time being.

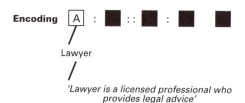

Figure 3.8

Stage 2: Inference
When the solver sees 'Client' (the B term) for the first time the encoding component would be triggered again (Figure 3.9). Let's assume that 'Client is a person who uses a professional person's services' is retrieved from LTM and stored in WM when 'Client' is encoded.

We also hypothesize an *inference* process that works out and stores in WM a relation between the A and B terms, 'Lawyer' and 'Client', when they are presented together in a context such as this. This component may involve quite complex memory processes, and we'll come back to this in due course, but for the moment let's assume that the relation inferred is 'provides legal advice' which, as a link between the first two terms, gives us 'Lawyer provides legal advice for Client', as shown in Figure 3.9.

Figure 3.9

Stage 3: Mapping

When the third term, 'Doctor', is presented, encoding again occurs (Figure 3.10). Presumably what is retrieved when the third term is encoded must be influenced by the activation resulting from previous stages. Let's assume that 'Doctor is a licenced professional who provides medical advice' is retrieved from LTM and stored in WM along with all the other information retrieved up to this point (in the rest of this series of diagrams, the encoded features stored in WM are signified by the series of dots at the end of the pointers from different terms, as in Figure 3.10).

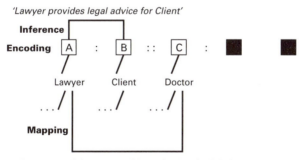

Figure 3.10

Figure 3.10 also depicts the mapping component, which follows on from the encoding of the C term. Mapping is the component that links the domain of the analogy to the range. Another way to look at this is to say that mapping finds links between two different domains

115

indicated by the A and C terms — in this case the domains of Lawyers and Doctors.

Again, ignoring the complexity of the memory search that might be involved in this, let's assume that the solver thinks of Lawyers and Doctors as both being people who 'provide professional advice' and stores such a relation in WM.

Stage 4: Application
In Figure 3.11 we show both solution alternatives as having already been encoded, in order to save space. We assume that something like 'a place where the sick and injured are treated' and 'someone in the care of a doctor' are retrieved from LTM and stored in WM after encoding for 'Hospital' and 'Patient', respectively.

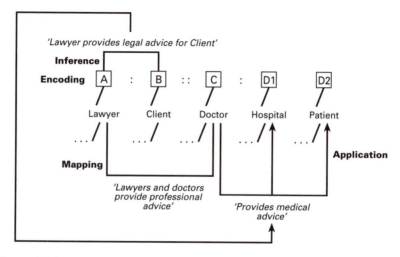

Figure 3.11

Figure 3.11 also shows the terms involved in the application component. In essence, a relation isomorphic to the relation already inferred between the first two terms of the analogy is applied to the C term to derive a solution that can then be matched to each of the solution terms in turn. The inferred relation between 'Lawyer' and 'Client', remember, was 'provides legal advice', so a similar relation might be 'provides medical advice' for application from 'Doctor' to the two alternatives. The tests to follow would then be (a) 'Doctor provides medical advice to Hospital', and (b) 'Doctor provides medical advice to Patient'. Doctors don't advise hospitals on their medical condition, so we assume here that the D1 alternative is rejected, and the application component tries again with the second alternative, which the solver would (hopefully) recognize as the correct alternative.

Stage 5: Justification
In addition to the components outlined above — encoding, inference, mapping, and application — Sternberg proposed a *justification* component. When problems are presented in a forced-choice format, there will be cases when solvers think that none of the completion terms is ideally acceptable, and are forced to choose what they regard to be the best of a bad lot. This 'best guess' process is what Sternberg calls the justification component. (When problems are presented in a true/false format, if no second order relation can be found linking the two parts of the analogy, then the solver will be left to think that a false analogy has been presented.)

Stage 6: Response
Finally, we need a *response* component that enables the solver to announce the solution to the problem. In fact, the response component is actually a preparation/response component, as it contains elements of preparation (e.g. strategic planning) as well as responding.

4.2   Models of reasoning strategies

We can now discuss ways in which this small set of processing components might be organized into different strategies for solving analogies, and how differences in strategies might be related to different people's ability to solve analogies. Thus far, we have discussed analogy solution as a rather straightforward process; we assumed that only a very small number of facts were available to the solver, and for purposes of explication we assumed that only facts that led directly to a solution (Lawyer provides legal advice for Client; Doctor provides medical advice for Patient; Doctor and Lawyer provide professional advice to Client and Patient, respectively) were retrieved and stored in WM. In reality however, a large amount of information about lawyers, clients, doctors, medicine and patients might be accessed and potentially used by a solver presented with such a problem. When we consider all the knowledge that *might* be brought to bear at any one point in time, we are immediately confronted with the question of how people organize solution processes. We can show this with reference to an example discussed by Sternberg (1977), who mooted and tested four different possible strategies.

The models involve the same six performance components: encoding, inference, mapping, application, justification, and response. The four models we describe differ in terms of whether inference, mapping and application processes are *exhaustive* (i.e. each process uses all of the information available in working memory before another process is initiated, as further described below) or *self-terminating* (i.e. each process uses the first piece of information available in working memory and then initiates the next process), and with respect to whether the application process (whether exhaustive or self-terminating) involves *sequential option scanning* or *alternating option scanning* (these aspects of the different models are not shown in Table 3.1, but are described below). In Table 3.1, E is used to indicate an exhaustive process, and S to indicate self-termination.

Table 3.1   Sternberg's strategy models for analogical reasoning

	Model 1	Model 2	Model 3	Model 4
Inference	E	E	E	S
Mapping	E	E	S	S
Application	E	S	S	S

Model 1 is the most complex, in that the inference, mapping and application components are all exhaustive, and so the description of Model 1 will be fairly detailed. You may feel tempted to skim over some of these details. However, the section yields to one careful reading. You are advised to put an effort into reading carefully about Model 1, as such care will make it a lot easier to understand the other three models.

Our example problem is this: Washington:1::Lincoln: (a) 10 (b) 5. This particular problem would not be likely to appear in a British test, since its solution requires a little knowledge about America that the ordinary British subject would not be expected to have. This knowledge includes the facts that:

1 Washington was an American president (the first).
2 Washington was a war hero.
3 Washington's portrait appears on the one dollar bill.
4 Lincoln was also a president (the sixteenth).
5 Lincoln was a war hero.
6 Lincoln's portrait appears on the 5 dollar bill.

Thus, the correct alternative in the analogy problem is '(b) 5' (i.e. both Washington and Lincoln have their portraits on US currency). Armed with this little bit of knowledge, we can now proceed, but first let us recap what we have said about the processes involved in the model. During encoding, information related to each term is retrieved from LTM and stored in WM. The inference component determines the relation between the A and B terms of the analogy. Mapping involves working out the relationship between the A and C terms of the analogy (the domain and range of the analogy). Application involves applying information about the A:B relation to the C term to derive a solution.

The justification component is employed when the solver is not sure about a solution to the problem. The response component, of course, is used to announce a decision.

Model 1
In this model, inference, mapping and application are all exhaustive processes (as shown in Table 3.1) operating in the sequence in which they've been named.

Encoding: The first thing that happens is that 'Washington' is encoded. Let's assume that the following facts are retrieved and stored in WM during encoding (see Table 3.2): Washington was the first US president; Washington's portrait is on the US currency; Washington was a Revolutionary War hero. The representation in Table 3.2 organizes all this information in terms of *object-attribute-value triples*. Thus, in the first encoding for Washington in Table 3.2, Washington is the object, president is an attribute of Washington, and first is the value for this particular attribute. The same representation is used throughout this section.

Table 3.2   Encoding: Washington

Washington (president (first))
Washington (portrait is on US currency (one dollar))
Washington (war hero (Revolutionary War))

Next, the solver reads '1' and encodes it (lets argue) as shown in Table 3.3.

Table 3.3   Encoding: 1

1 (counting number (one))
1 (ordinal position (first))
1 (amount (one unit))

Inference: Once the A and B terms have been encoded, the inference component would be triggered as the next process in the sequence. Since in this model inference is exhaustive, it uses all of the information in WM about the A and B terms in order to determine relations between them. Thus, all three facts about Washington would be matched with every fact about 1 in order to determine what relation(s) can be established. In short, we want to know if the two objects, Washington and 1 (in our object-attribute-value representation) have anything in common. One of the things they have in common is that they both have the *value* 'first', as shown here:

Washington (president   (**first**))
1   (ordinal position   (**first**))

(i.e. Washington was the *first* US president, and 1 is the *first* ordinal position).

Because of this shared value, the attribute 'ordinal position' for the object '1' is appended to the attribute 'president' for the object 'Washington', which yields:

Washington (president (ordinal position (first))).

Table 3.4 shows the sequence of matches between WM elements in Tables 3.2 and 3.3 that would be attempted through exhaustive inference. Note that (1(b)) and (2(c)) would be the only two elements that would succeed. The new additions to WM would be the following:

Washington (president (ordinal position (first))).
Washington (portrait on US currency (amount (one unit))).

Table 3.4 Sequence of successful matches between WM elements in Tables 3.2 and 3.3 resulting from exhaustive inference

(1)
(a)	Washington	(president	(first))
	1	(counting number	(one))
(b)	Washington	(president	(first))
	1	(ordinal position	(first))
(c)	Washington	(president	(first))
	1	(amount	(one unit))

(2)
(a)	Washington	(portrait is on US currency	(one unit))
	1	(counting number	(one))
(b)	Washington	(portrait is on US currency	(one unit))
	1	(ordinal position	(first))
(c)	Washington	(portrait is on US currency	(one unit))
	1	(amount	(one unit))

(3)
(a)	Washington	(war hero	(Revolutionary War))
	1	(counting number	(one))
(b)	Washington	(war hero	(Revolutionary War))
	1	(ordinal position	(first))
(c)	Washington	(war hero	(Revolutionary War))
	1	(amount	(one unit))

Mapping: Let's assume that encoding of Lincoln (Table 3.5) leads to the generation of facts isomorphic to those retrieved for Washington.

Table 3.5   Encoding: Lincoln

Lincoln (president (sixteenth))
Lincoln (portrait on US currency (5 dollars))
Lincoln (war hero (Civil War))

After encoding, the mapping component attempts to discover links between the A (Washington) and C (Lincoln) terms. The results of exhaustive matching — that both Washington and Lincoln were presidents, have their portrait on US currency and were war heroes — are shown in Table 3.6. (You should be able to assure yourself of the veridicality of these matches by applying the same procedure outlined in the section on inference, above.)

Table 3.6   Mapping: Washington:Lincoln

Washington and Lincoln (presidents (ordinal position (first, sixteenth)))
Washington and Lincoln (portraits on US currency (1 and 5 dollar bills))
Washington and Lincoln (war heroes (Revolutionary and Civil Wars))

Exhaustive application: In the next step, the two answer options are encoded, and the facts shown in Table 3.7 are generated.

Table 3.7   Encoding: 10,5

---

10 (counting number (ten))
10 (ordinal position (tenth))
10 (amount (ten units))
 5 (counting number (five))
 5 (ordinal position (fifth))
 5 (amount (five units))

Now the solver would try to apply a relation between Lincoln and 10 which is consonant with information inferred and stored earlier about relations between Washington and 1. The relations inferred between Washington and 1 were 'Washington (president (ordinal position (first)))' and 'Washington (portrait on US currency (amount (one unit)))', so application involves applying 'Lincoln president' and 'Lincoln portrait on US currency' to 10 and 5 to see if one of them provides a satisfactory completion. Application can occur in one of two modes — *sequential option scanning* or *alternating option scanning*. In sequential option scanning, all inferences are applied from Lincoln to all the facts retrieved about 10 before they are applied to the facts about 5 (see Table 3.8a). In alternating option scanning, the first inference is applied from Lincoln to 10 and then 5 in turn, and so on for each inference available to the solver (see Table 3.8b).

Table 3.8a   Exhaustive application using sequential option scanning

Lincoln president 10th	NIL
Lincoln portrait on US currency 10 dollars	NIL
Lincoln war hero 10th	NIL
Lincoln president 5th	NIL
Lincoln portrait on US currency 5 dollars	OK
Lincoln war hero 5th	NIL

Table 3.8b   Exhaustive application using alternating option scanning

Lincoln president 10th	NIL
Lincoln president 5th	NIL
Lincoln portrait on US currency 10 dollars	NIL
Lincoln portrait on US currency 5 dollars	OK
Lincoln war hero 10th	NIL
Lincoln war hero 5th	NIL

Justification and *response* then follow.

Note that in these two different modes of application, the solution to this particular problem would be found earlier in alternating option scanning than in sequential option scanning (fourth application as opposed to the fifth, respectively). In a model where all processes are exhaustive, such as Model 1, this wouldn't make any difference to response time, but in the other models described below, in which some processes are self-terminating, there would be a difference.

Model 2

Model 2 is exactly the same as Model 1, except that application, the last process in the chain, is a self-terminating process. Since encoding, inferring and mapping are the same as in Model 1, all of the information available to a solver using that model is also available to a person using this model (see Tables 3.2 to 3.7). But when it comes to application, the solver using the Model 2 strategy only tests as many completions as necessary to come to a unique solution.

Model 3

Model 3 differs from Model 1 in that only the inference process is exhaustive, while both mapping and application are self-terminating. Thus, all the information given in Tables 3.2 to 3.5 would be available to the solver when mapping begins, but at this point the solver would make only the first mapping given in Table 3.6, and then try to apply the inference inhering in the first mapping to each of the solution alternatives. If no unique solution were found, the solver would again try the mapping component and then application (the solution terms have already been encoded so would not need to be re-encoded).

Model 4

Model 4 is the other extreme strategic model — almost the exact opposite of Model 1 — in that in Model 4 inference, mapping and application are all self-terminating rather than exhaustive. Thus, under this model, after encoding Washington and 1 (as in Tables 3.2 and 3.3), the solver would make an inference (such as the first successful inference in Table 3.4), then encode Lincoln, then do the first mapping, then encode the solution options, and finally apply the known inference and respond if a solution is found.

4.3   Experimental tests of models

Now that we have a number of possible strategies, our next problem is to determine which one(s) people actually use when they are presented with analogies. This section is concerned with describing one method in which different models can be tested.

Suppose I gave you the following analogy to solve:

Candle:Tallow::Tyre: (a) Automobile (b) Rubber

and found that it took you fifteen seconds to respond with the correct answer. How could we use this reaction time data in order to tell us something about the individual component processes — encoding, inference, mapping, application, justification and response — involved in the solution? The answer is that, as it stands, we couldn't. We just don't know how the total fifteen seconds was divided up between the component processes.

Now consider the following experimental set-up. In one condition I present you with a number of analogies as above, and calculate your average response time. In other conditions I present you with analogies in two parts. In the first part, when you indicate that you are ready, I present, say,

Canine

and give you all the time you need in order to encode the presented stimulus. I note the time from the presentation of the stimulus to the instant you indicate that you are ready for the second part. When you are ready to continue, I present the whole analogy:

Canine:Dog::Equine: (a) Goat (b) Horse.

As soon as you know the answer (but taking as much time as you need) you respond by pressing an appropriate answer key. So now I have measured two reaction times: (1) the time to *encode* 'Canine' (a single term of the analogy), and (2) the time to complete the whole task, involving all the processes, including further instances of encoding. This is an example of *pre-cueing*, in which different subtasks (or different numbers of terms of the full analogy) of the complete task are given in the first part of the experiment and the full task in the second part. In this way, we can find out how much time is allocated to each component of the task. The response time for the pre-cued part of the task (to encode 'Canine' in this example) is the *cue score*, and the response time for the second part of the task (the whole task in this example) is the *solution score*.

Examples of all four conditions, in which 0, 1, 2 or 3 cues are given in the pre-cuing part of the experiment, are given in Table 3.9.

Table 3.9

0 cues:	Legislator:Lobbyist::Jury: (a) Lawyer (b) Judge	*solution score:*
1 cue:	Raincoat	*cue score:*
	Raincoat:Rain::Foxhole: (a) Foxes (b) Gunfire	*solution score:*
2 cues:	Spouse:Husband	*cue score:*
	Spouse:Husband::Sibling: (a) Uncle (b) Brother	*solution score:*
3 cues:	Uncle:Nephew::Aunt	*cue score:*
	Uncle:Nephew::Aunt: (a) Niece (b) Cousin	*solution score:*

Note that in the 1 cue condition, it is possible to isolate the time for encoding the A term, because it is assumed that only encoding occurs during the pre-cuing stage of the experiment with one cue. Subjects may participate in hundreds or even thousands of trials in each condition of the experiment, and the average time over all the trials is taken to indicate the time a particular subject needs for encoding. For the sake of argument, let's say that an individual takes an average (over hundreds or thousands of trials) of three seconds to encode an item. So we can say that encoding = 3 seconds per term on any given analogy problem.

In the 2 cue condition, in which both the A and B terms are presented together, inference can be isolated during the pre-cuing stage by subtracting out the average time needed for encoding, times two (since both the A and B terms are encoded in this condition). The amount of time remaining after the time for encoding has been removed is assumed to be the amount of time needed for inferencing. So, if, on average, an individual takes 10 seconds to complete the 2 cue condition, then inference can be said to require 4 seconds because encoding the A and B terms should take 6 seconds altogether (encoding

= 3 seconds, times 2 terms), which, when subtracted from the 10 seconds spent on this task leaves 4 seconds for the inference process.

In the 3 cue condition, mapping can be isolated by subtracting out the time needed to encode the A, B and C terms (time for encoding, times three), plus the time needed for inferring a relation between the A and B terms (a time isolated in the 2 cue condition, above). The time remaining is the time needed for mapping the A and C terms.

In the 0 cue condition, time required for the only process not yet isolated — application — can be estimated after subtracting out the time for the processes isolated in the other conditions.

Sternberg used the reaction-time data in two different ways. First, the data was used to determine whether different groups of solvers used different strategies, described as Models 1 to 4 in Section 4.2. Secondly, he used reaction-time data to distinguish between good and poor solvers on the component processes used in solving analogies. The data was analysed using a mathematical modelling technique called regression analysis, the details of which needn't concern us.

The results showed that there was no reliable difference in the strategy used by subjects in different ability groups. Model 3, in which inference is exhaustive and mapping and application are both self-terminating, accounted for most of the variance. Sternberg found greatest support for Model 3 on the people-piece and verbal analogies, but the distinction between Models 3 and 4 was very thin indeed. In fact, in announcing what really amounts to a personal preference for Model 3 over Model 4, Sternberg could only claim: '[The] data indicate that application is *almost certainly* self-terminating, mapping is *most probably* self-terminating, and inference *may be* exhaustive, although here the distinction [between Models 3 and 4] is unclear' (italics mine). The data also supported alternating option scanning as the likeliest application strategy for all subjects.

This seems to be a remarkable finding, because it indicates that there are no differences between people who are good and people who are poor at analogical reasoning at the level of procedural knowledge — knowledge about how to do analogical reasoning. Since one model is claimed to account for the performances of people from different ability groups, they must all be doing the same thing in solving such problems. We shall discuss this claim again in Section 6, which describes more recent research on reasoning strategies.

Sternberg did find differences in the amount of time people from different ability groups spent on the component processes in solving analogy problems. Specifically, he found that good reasoners spend significantly less time than poorer reasoners on inference and mapping when solving verbal and geometric analogies (but not on people-piece analogies); they spend less time on application in the geometric analogies (but not on either people-piece or verbal analogies); and they also spend less time on the response component (which Sternberg suggests contains an element of solution planning that has not been isolated in any of his models discussed in the previous section) on all three types of analogies.

Interestingly, Sternberg found that the better reasoners spent *more* time on encoding than poor reasoners. This finding is counterintuitive because it suggests that the smarter you are, the longer it takes you to understand a problem. Sternberg argued that, in fact, spending more time on encoding is a superior strategy in that later processes like inferencing, mapping and application can run off more efficiently (quickly) if a good problem representation, or encoding, has been achieved. In Part II we saw that one of the ways in which novices and experts differ when solving problems is in the nature of the problem representation they construct. We saw that some representations facilitated problem solving while other representations might even preclude finding a solution. So this is one point at which strands of analogical problem solving and analogical reasoning research have come together.

It was also suggested in Part II that the nature of a novice's or expert's problem representation is a function of knowledge — experts have more knowledge and the knowledge they have is better organized. Whether or not it is the case that good and poor solvers in analogical reasoning differ with respect to the amount and organization of their verbal/conceptual knowledge has not been addressed in the research presented in this section, but I shall have more to say about the role of such factors in analogical reasoning in Section 4.4 and in the evaluation of this research in Section 6.

To summarize, Sternberg did not find differences between people in different ability groups in terms of the processes or strategies they used, but he did find differences in the amount of time needed by people in the different groups to run off the individual processes. Good reasoners spend more time on encoding, but less time on inference, mapping and application processes.

4.4   The role of task factors in analogical reasoning

Word meanings
Heller (1979) pointed out that Sternberg's research was based on the reaction times of highly intelligent University students solving relatively simple problems, while what we are interested in is the modelling of performances by widely different skill groups on problems with wide-ranging levels of difficulty; and that evidence for Sternberg's model was weakest for verbal analogies. Heller drew attention to several

variables that need to be considered in research that aims at a more realistic account of differences between people who are good and those who are not so good at analogical reasoning. First, the words used in verbal analogies are obviously important. If you're confronted with a problem with four terms that are not a part of your vocabulary or experience, then the problem might as well be presented in a foreign language that you don't understand. If you didn't know what US dollar bills are like you could not have done the Washington/Lincoln problem. It would essentially be a vocabulary test rather than a test of your reasoning abilities.

With word stimuli, it is impossible for an experimenter to characterize or quantify all of the features that might be involved in an encoding process, even for so-called simple words like 'green' and 'sparrow'. For one thing, the context of the encoding should have an impact on the kind and number of features encoded. When we see a word like 'Lawyer' in one of these analogy tasks, do we retrieve all possible features of the word from our internal lexicon, or just a few features determined by the local context? This is an important concern because, in a given list of analogy problems, encoding of some words may take two, five, or ten times longer than the encoding of other words.

This was not so much of a problem on the geometric and people-piece analogies used in Sternberg's research because difficulty of encoding and other components could be directly manipulated by varying the number of elements and their dimensions and the number and kind of transformations involved in sets of problems. But for verbal stimuli, it is generally not possible to say beforehand how many features need to be encoded, except intuitively. For example, the encoding stage for the analogy 'Bird:Sparrow::Fish:Salmon' probably doesn't require much of an extended featural representation of the different terms, since in both the domain and the range of the analogy the second term simply names a subset of the first. An easy problem. On the other hand, encoding the terms of 'Hawk:Fierce::Kestrel:Elegant' probably requires considerable featural encoding of the different terms before the correct relationships can be generated and compared. Complexity or abstractness of the word concepts that are presented in different analogies just compounds the problem. Consider this analogy:

Quixotic:Feasible::Theoretical: (a) Practical (b) Workable

Which of the alternatives is the correct answer? What does 'quixotic' mean? The unsolved problem of completely understanding how words are represented in human memory points up the amount of magic inhering in a term like 'encoding' and limits the depth to which we are able to explore details of the processes in which we are interested.

Relational features

Another important variable is the nature of the relation that occurs between the terms of an analogy. Consider this pair of analogies:

Green:Emerald::Red: ?

Ear:Hear::Eye: ?

Each of these problems involves a different type of relation. In the first, there is a 'property' relation, whereby green and red are colour properties of emeralds and rubies, respectively. In the second, there is a 'function' relation, whereby hearing is a function of ears, seeing of eyes. Normally, intelligence tests consist of a large number of verbal analogies composed from a relatively small number of different relation types.

Activity 13

Here's another set of problems. See if you can identify and name different relation types for the problems as you solve them. Note that problems 5 and 7 have already been described as having a 'property' relation and 'function' relation, respectively. It's up to you to dream up a name for any different type of relation you perceive between the terms of the different analogies.

1   Biology:Science::Sculpture: ?
2   Wolf:Dog::Tiger: ?
3   Paragraph:Sentence::Sentence: ?
4   Acorn:Oak::Bulb: ?
5   Green:Emerald::Red: ?
6   Man:Bread::Horse: ?
7   Ear:Hear::Eye: ?
8   Sail:Cloth::Oar: ?
9   Butter:Bread::Sugar: ?
10 Train:Rails:Automobile: ?
11 Car:Brakes::Ship: ?

A number of researchers have analysed analogy problems in standard intelligence tests, such as the Cognitive Abilities Test (CAT) or the Graduate Records Examination (GRE), in order to try to catalogue the range of different relations commonly found (Whiteley, 1976; Whiteley and Dawis, 1974; Pellegrino and Glaser, 1982). The list provided in Table 3.10 is from Pellegrino and Glaser (1982).

The influence of relation type in analogical reasoning has been investigated in experiments by Whiteley and Dawis (1974). In this study, experimental subjects were classified as good or poor at analogical reasoning on the basis of previous ability scores. Both groups were

Table 3.10   Examples of analogy relation types (Pellegrino and Glaser, 1982)

Relation type	Definition	Analogy example
Class member	(a) One term is a specific instance of the (more general) other term	Biology:Science::Sculpture:
	(b) Both terms are instances of a more general class	Wolf:Dog::Tiger:
Part-whole	One term is a part of the other	Paragraph:Sentence:: Sentence:
Order	One term always follows the other in time	Acorn:Oak::Bulb:
Property	One term has the property or quality defined by the other	Green:Emerald::Red:
Function	(a) One term performs some function for or action on the other	Man:Bread::Horse:
	(b) One term performs the function defined by the other term	Ear:Hear::Eye:
Conversion	One term is made from or is a product of the other	Sail:Cloth::Oar:
Location	(a) One term is located in, on, or about the other often or always	Butter:Bread::Sugar:
	(b) One term performs some activity in, on, or about the other often or always	Train:Rails::Automobile:
Part-whole and function	One term is a part of the other and performs a specialized function	Car:Brakes::Ship:

provided with the 'appropriate relational concept' along with each problem they were asked to solve. Not only did this manipulation facilitate problem solution, but it was also shown that poor solvers dramatically increased their ability scores on subsequent tests.

In subsequent research, Whiteley (1976) hypothesized that people who are good at solving analogies might not only be good at inferring relations, but (1) may educe more relations for a given pair of terms than less skilled solvers, and (2) may also be quicker at making such eductions. However, the research showed that there were no significant relationships between either number of relations or number of different types of relations inferred in the experimental task and measured level of analogical reasoning ability: subjects from high and low ability groups inferred about the same number of relations and the same number of different relation types. Whiteley's prediction was not supported.

Table 3.11 shows associations between abilities (e.g. syllogistic reasoning and induction) and success with different types of analogy (e.g. opposites). Asterisks indicate a significant association. An interesting corollary of this research is that particular patterns of ability may be measured simply by devising tests that include only particular types of relation between terms. This would be particularly important if it were found that, say, associational fluency and divergent thinking abilities were particularly good predictors of success in (again say) the legal profession. It suggests that it would be possible to provide a rationale for including particular items on different tests. At the moment, however, inclusion of different items is often more a matter of caprice than of principled selection (Bejar, Chaffin, and Embretson, 1991).

Table 3.11   Correlation patterns between relational solution type and abilities (based on Whiteley, 1976)

	Associational fluency	Divergent thinking	Syllogistic reasoning	Associative memory	Induction	Semantic flexibility
(1) Opposites			*		*	
(2) Functional			*	*		*
(3) Word pattern	*	*				
(4) Similarities		*	*			
(5) Conversion		*	*			*

Summary of Section 4

- The earliest process model of analogical reasoning was put forward by Spearman, who theorized that such reasoning involved (a) the apprehension of experience, (b) eduction of relations, and (c) eduction of correlates.
- Sternberg expanded Spearman's model and named the component processes in analogical reasoning as (a) encoding, (b) inference, (c) mapping, (d) application, (e) justification, and (f) response.

- Sternberg used a pre-cueing (subtask) method of research to determine the amount of time subjects spent on each of the component processes involved in analogical reasoning. Pre-cueing involved presenting 0, 1, 2, or 3 terms of an analogy problem in the first part of the experiment and the full problem in the second part.
- Sternberg's research suggested that people with different abilities in analogical reasoning used the same overall solution strategy — exhaustive inference and self-terminating mapping and application — but that they differed in the amount of time spent on the component processes. Although the results were somewhat mixed between the different types of analogy problems, good solvers spent more time on encoding but less time on inference, mapping, application and response components. The extra time spent on encoding by good solvers is thought to result in a better elaborated problem representation which facilitates the operation of subsequent processes.
- Task factors such as word meaning and the relations between word pairs are important variables in analogical reasoning.

5   Analogical, buggy-analogical, and non-analogical solution strategies

Heller (1979) made clever use of think aloud protocols in her research on the solution behaviour of groups of subjects who differed in their analogical reasoning ability as measured by standard intelligence tests. Subjects were presented with forced-choice analogies in two stages. In the first stage subjects would see the stem of the analogy, and in the second stage they would see four alternative solution terms, one at a time. When subjects saw the stem they were probed by the experimenter for information, such as what they thought was the relation between the A and B terms. They were also probed for their thoughts as each solution alternative was presented. The subjects were allowed to see only one alternative at a time, but they could ask to re-view and re-consider previously seen alternatives at any time they wished. In all, Heller found three major types of solutions in the protocols of good, intermediate, and poor solvers. These types — analogical, buggy-analogical, and non-analogical — are described in the next three subsections.

5.1   Analogical solutions

Analogical solutions are those that contained no violations of task constraints (i.e. the solution involved finding a solution where the D alternative had the same (or closest) relationship to the C term as the B term had to the A term). Heller found that the behaviour of all solvers evinced their knowledge of task constraints at least part of the time. However, good solvers were much more consistent than intermediate and poor solvers, producing *analogical* solutions on nearly 100 per cent of the problems with which they were presented, while intermediate and poor solvers managed this on only 71 per cent and 34 per cent of problems, respectively. Intermediate and poor solvers produced other kinds of solutions, such as 'buggy analogical' (see below). Here is an example protocol from Heller's thesis illustrating an analogical solution in which one option matches the initial specification of the relation between the A and B terms of the analogy. (In the protocols that follow, S stands for subject and E stands for experimenter.)

Analogy problem: Tea : Coffee :: Bread: (a) Milk (b) Butter (c) Rolls (d) Jam

S: *(Considers the stem alone: Tea:Coffee::Bread:).* Tea is to coffee as bread is to ... rolls because tea and coffee, they're both drinks, and they're about the same thing, just two different names for two different drinks, and a bread and a roll would be about the same ... two different names for the same thing.

S: *(Considers option (a): Milk).* That doesn't fit, it's a drink.

S: *(Considers option (b): Butter).* Butter is something you put on bread, that doesn't fit.

S: *(Considers option (c): Rolls).* That's good.

S: *(Considers option (d): Jam).* It's like butter, something you put on bread. It wouldn't fit because you don't put coffee on tea or in tea.

5.2   Buggy-analogical solutions

A second type of solution was called *buggy analogical* ('buggy' is a term used in computer programming to indicate a faulty procedure). Buggy-analogical solutions were described as those that violated certain of the task constraints involved in analogical reasoning. An example of a buggy-analogical solution would be to determine that the A:B relation matched the C:D relation when in fact they did not match. This sort of behaviour was seen in the protocols of only 1 per cent of good solvers, but 13 per cent and 15 per cent of intermediate and poor solvers, respectively. An example (also from Heller) of a protocol in which a buggy-analogical solution is seen, is presented below. Notice that the solution is non-analogical initially, but becomes analogical when the subject notices the relationship between 'Circle' (the C term) and 'Compass' (the final alternative), and then compares that relation to the relation between 'Line' and 'Ruler' (the A and B terms).

Analogy problem: Line:Ruler::Circle: (a) Draw (b) Radius (c) Round (d) Compass

S: *(Considers the stem alone: Line:Ruler::Circle:)* Round. A circle's round.

S: *(Considers option (a): Draw)*. No. Draw could mean anything.

S: *(Considers option (b): Radius)*. Maybe, yeah. How big the circle is, like.

S: *(Considers option (c): Round)*. Yeah, I think that's good.

S: *(Considers option (d): Compass)*. Yeah, compass is good, because you use a ruler to draw a line, and you use a compass to draw a circle.

E: Which do you like best?

S: Compass, because you draw a circle with a compass, and a line with a ruler.

5.3   Non-analogical solutions

Non-analogical solutions included solutions where solvers failed to find (or search for) relations between word pairs in both the domain and range of an analogy, or used illegal pairings, such as looking for a relation between the A and D terms of a problem, and so on. None of the good solvers ever showed signs of non-analogical reasoning, but such patterns were found in the behaviour of 16 per cent and 50 per cent of intermediate and poor solvers, respectively. An example of a protocol in which a non-analogical solution is seen, involving identification of A:B and C:D relations but without consideration of the second order relation, is this:

Analogy problem: Tell : Listen :: Give: (a) Present (b) Lose (c) Get (d) Have

S: *(Considers the stem alone: Tell:Listen::Give:)* Take. If you tell something, they're like taking it in. If you give something, they take it.

S: *(Considers option (a): Present)*. Tell is to listen as give is to present? Yeah, I'd go with that! You give presents.

S: *(Considers option (b): Lose)*. No. Most people find something, they ain't gonna give it back.

S: *(Considers option (c): Get)*. Get. Yeah. If you get something, somebody gave it to you.

S: *(Considers option (d): Have)*. When they give it to you, you have it. Yeah.

E: Which of these do you think is best?

S: Present. Because you give presents.

SAQ 18
In this last protocol the subject accepts options (a), (c), and (d) during the course of solution, but, after probing by the experimenter, chooses option (a) as the best solution. Which solution would you have chosen? Why?

What is the nature of the relationship between the C term of the analogy and the solver's 'solution' ('Take'), mentioned by the solver immediately after seeing the stem of the analogy?

5.4   Conceptual and interactive strategies

Heller's research indicated that two different analogical reasoning strategies were needed to characterize subjects' performance adequately, depending upon both problem difficulty and skill level. One model, which Heller called a *conceptual model*, was able to account for the performance of adult solvers of all skill levels on 'easy' problems. The conceptual model is similar to Sternberg's model, in that the same processes are employed, but differs in the sequencing of solution processes. Under the conceptual model, encoding occurs for each term of the analogy, as in the Sternberg model, but inferencing occurs between the C term and each alternative solution option as well as between the A and B terms. Mapping is missing from this model but is replaced by a *comparison component*.

The sequence of processing under the conceptual model is as follows:

1 the solver encodes and infers a relation between the A and B terms;
2 the solver then encodes and infers a relation between the C term and each solution option, in turn; and
3 the solver then compares the relations between C and each of the D alternatives for similarity to the relation inferred between the A and B terms. The relation providing the closest match wins, and the associated solution term is selected. A generalized model of the solution process under the conceptual model is presented in Figure 3.12.

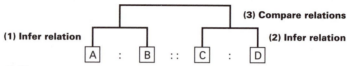

Figure 3.12

The major difference between Sternberg's model and Heller's is that in Heller's model the solver works out a *relation* between the C term and each solution alternative and each of these *relations* is compared with the *relation* previously inferred between the A and B terms. In Sternberg's model, a *generate-and-test* procedure is employed: once the relation between the A and B terms has been inferred, that relation is applied to the C term to generate an ideal solution (the *generate* part of the procedure) and that ideal is compared to each of the solution alternatives in turn (the *test* part of the procedure).

To give a concrete example of Heller's conceptual model, the processing sequence for the analogy 'Lawyer:Client::Doctor: (a) Hospital (b) Patient' would be as follows. The first thing to happen would be that the A and B terms would be encoded and a relation inferred between them ('advises', say). Next, the C term and the first solution option ('Hospital') would be encoded and a relation inferred ('works in', say). The two relations would then be compared for a match, which in this case would fail because there doesn't seem to be much in common between 'advises' and 'works in'. At the next step, the C term is again encoded, as is the next solution option ('Patient'), and a relation inferred ('advises', say, for purposes of simplification). The comparison process would find this an exact match and the analogy would be solved.

In Figure 3.13 a somewhat more realistic version of the conceptual model for the solution of the 'Lawyer:Client::Doctor' problem is presented. Notice that, in the figure, the relations identified are 'provides legal advice' and 'provides medical advice', respectively. Thus, the comparison process involves a bit more processing than a direct match of exact relations; the reasoner has to decide that the two relations are close enough in meaning (e.g. 'provide professional advice') for the solution alternative to be correct.

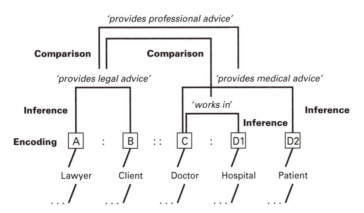

Figure 3.13

As a quick reminder, under Sternberg's model, the inferred relation ('provides legal advice') between the A (Lawyer) and B (Client) terms would be applied to the C term to generate an ideal solution ('Doctor provides medical advice to patient'). The solution term would then be checked against the alternatives for a match.

Activity 14
Go back to Section 5.1 and consider again the protocol presented there.
Is this evidence for Heller's conceptual model? If not, why not?

This does not look like evidence for Heller's conceptual model. Under Heller's conceptual model the subject should consider the C term and each solution term in turn, work out a relation, and compare that relation with the relation worked out for the A and B terms. If the relations match, the subject should choose the option as the correct one; if not, then the subject should move on to the next option and repeat the original process. But what the subject does is generate an ideal solution term — 'Rolls' — and then go through the list testing each alternative against the ideal solution. This is like Sternberg's model, not Heller's. This fact draws our attention to the need to be extremely careful about how protocols are used, if you use them; it also draws attention to the fact that you should not accept an analysis of a verbal protocol without going through it yourself, with an attitude of scepticism.

Both Sternberg's generate-and-test model and Heller's conceptual model are pretty algorithmic; they are like recipes for solving analogies. However, Heller also proposed a second, *interactive model* in which the processing sequence depended upon (a) how far a solver got before running into difficulties, and (b) skill level. Good solvers provided more evidence for interactive processing than did poor solvers. In order to illustrate Heller's interactive model, consider yourself faced with the following problem:

Quixotic:Feasible::Theoretical: (a) Practical (b) Workable

For the sake of argument, let's say that you don't understand the meaning of 'Quixotic', and so can't work out a definite relation between 'Quixotic' and 'Feasible', the A and B terms, as a first step. One way you could proceed would be to look at the C term ('Theoretical') in conjunction with each of the solution alternatives ('Practical' and 'Workable') to see if you could work out any relations there. Let's imagine that when you consider 'Theoretical' and 'Practical' together, you vaguely remember an old saying along the lines 'That guy's all theory and no practice'. This suggests a relation of 'opposites' or 'one or the other' to you. So you return to the A and B pair to see if you can make 'opposite' fit. But you still don't know what 'Quixotic' means, so you can't be sure. So now you go back to the C term again and try to find a relation between 'Theoretical' and 'Workable'. You consider ways in which being theoretical and being workable might be alike. Assume that you think 'Well, maybe things go from being theoretical in the first place and only workable later'. This suggests a sort of time sequence relation between the two. So again you return to the A and B terms to see if you can make that relation fit. But since you still don't known what 'Quixotic' means, you're stuck again. What next? Maybe you could get some useful information from a comparison of the A and C terms, or the B and D terms? You might suddenly think of Don Quixote the next time you look at the A term. Whether or not that helps will depend upon what you know about this great fictional character. In the end, we can't say what would actually happen, but you might end up just guessing the answer (and you'll have a 50 per cent chance of being right, of course).

In the interactive model, there is considerable recursive processing (i.e. employment of the same process again and again) and comparison of pairs of terms, which was not seen in Sternberg's model or in Heller's conceptual model. For example, good solvers will use relations discovered between the C term and solution alternatives in order to reformulate earlier decisions about the relation between the A and B terms. Good solvers return to reprocess A–B terms or decide to abandon processing of A–B terms in favour of processing A–C terms when they get stuck. The results also show that there is a slight difference in favour of good solvers in the amount of time spent on processing the first three terms of an analogy, but that good solvers are significantly quicker in selecting a solution alternative in forced-choice analogies. This finding suggests that, in a given amount of time, good solvers probably encode more attributes of the different terms of an analogy and make more inferences. This early 'lead' in processing the stem of the analogy enables good solvers to make quick decisions on solution alternatives.

SAQ 19
Go back to Sections 5.1, 5.2 and 5.3 and re-read the protocols presented at the end of each section. Which of the solutions would you describe as conceptual and which as interactive? Why?

Summary of Section 5

- Heller identified three types of solutions in research involving people who were classified as good, intermediate or poor at analogical reasoning. The first type, analogical solutions, contained no violations of task constraints. This type of solution was characteristic of good solvers. The second type, buggy-analogical solutions, did contain certain violations of task constraints. The third type, non-analogical solutions, contained little but violations of task constraints. The second and third types of solution were found more often in the intermediate and poor solvers, respectively.

- Heller proposed two different models of analogical reasoning strategies, a conceptual model and an interactive model. Heller's conceptual model is similar to Sternberg's generate-and-test model, except that in Heller's model there is a relation comparison process instead of the application process in Sternberg's model (whereby solvers use the relation between the A and B terms of the analogy to generate an ideal solution, which is then tested against each solution term in turn). The evidence for Heller's conceptual model (even her own evidence) seems to be weaker than that for Sternberg's generate-and-test model.
- Heller found that the conceptual model characterized the behaviour of subjects at all skill levels on easy problems. However, the good solvers were more likely than intermediate and poor solvers to use interactive processing when they became stuck, usually when difficult problems were presented.
- According to the interactive model, good solvers will try different ways of tackling difficult problems. Good solvers may decide to abandon processing the A–B terms in favour of processing A–C or C–D terms when they get stuck. If that helps, they return to reprocess A–B terms. Again, one could quibble with Heller's evidence for the interactive model.

6   Conclusions

6.1   Recent advances

One of the overall aims of the componential approach, as outlined by Pellegrino and Glaser (1982) and quoted in Section 2.2, was to 'identify classes of test tasks that have consistently appeared on scholastic aptitude tests and use current techniques of task analysis to understand the nature of the performance elicited by these tasks'. Componential analysis represents an important initiative in pursuit of this goal. We have seen that a great deal of research has been conducted in order to identify the component processes underlying analogical reasoning. Robert Sternberg was one of the main instigators of this approach. Others have built upon the early attempts to model analogical reasoning and have contributed new insights through their own research. There is good agreement among different research groups on the nature of these processes, although they disagree about individual strategies and differences in the strategies that people employ across ability groups.

Sternberg and Gardner (1980) have extended their research to a range of other inductive reasoning tasks (e.g. *classification problems*). As with analogical reasoning problems, series completion problems consist of a stem from which the solver has to infer a rule for the relations between the terms in the stem and then complete the series. An example of a series completion problem would be: a c b d .... Sternberg and Gardner were able to show that inference, mapping and application are related to measured intelligence on a range of such tasks, and similar results have been found in experiments by Pellegrino and Glaser (1982).

Sternberg (1984) has elaborated his theory of intelligence well beyond the 1977 version discussed above and has added a role for social intelligence and learning processes to the originally postulated purely cognitive performance components. Sternberg has also made an attempt, in *Intelligence Applied: Understanding and Increasing your Intellectual Skills* (1986), to show how people can use his new theory to improve their intellectual performance in everyday problem-solving situations. This book discusses Sternberg's revised theory in some detail and provides the reader with activities designed to give them practice in applying what they learn to a wide range of problems, including everyday problems found outside the psychological laboratory. The following quotation from the first chapter of the book will give you a flavour of Sternberg's approach — and of his commitment to some of the ideas presented earlier in Part III:

> ... the preoccupation with testing [intelligence] was based on certain assumptions, at least one of which — that intelligence is, for the most part, a fixed and immutable characteristic — was seriously in error. ... the preoccupation with testing and the assumption that intelligence is a fixed entity led to a neglect of two possibly more important and productive questions: 'Can intelligence be trained, and if so, how?' This neglect was unfortunate, because the answer to the first question is yes. What this section will focus on is the second question: 'How?'

6.2 *Does analogical reasoning ability predict classroom performance?*

How do the models that have come out of analogical reasoning research relate to what is known about analogical problem solving in classroom settings? This question is important because it interacts with another of Pellegrino and Glaser's research goals which involves the issue of training intelligence so that people can perform better in academic settings. Let's remind ourselves of their exact words: 'A logical next step would be to relate the aptitude processes to similar task analytic work being pursued in school subject matter areas, e.g. beginning reading, text comprehension, elementary arithmetic, science problem solving, etc.'

Alexander, White, Haensley and Crimmins-Jeanes (1987) took a direct approach to the application of componential models of analogical reasoning to school subject areas. They argued that inferential text comprehension (i.e. the ability of readers to infer the meanings of words from surrounding context) involved all of the components identified by Sternberg in his model of analogical reasoning, and that training in these components should impact on a student's text understanding. In their study, Alexander *et al.* taught 10-year-olds how to solve proportional analogies, making sure that they understood the need to find relations between the A and B terms, the C and D terms, and to compare them. They even gave the children practice in making up their own analogies for the experimenter to solve. They found that this training significantly increased the children's ability to solve analogies, even after a considerable time lapse in which no further training was given, but they failed to find any evidence that the training helped children in inferential text understanding. A disappointing result.

Novick and Holyoak (1991) used subjects' Scholastic Aptitude Test scores as a measure of their mathematical ability, and the Differential Aptitude Tests as a measure of their analogical reasoning ability. They presented subjects with mathematics problems designed to test for transfer of learning from an example problem to later exercise problems. They wanted to find out whether skill in mathematics (which had been measured on the math section of the Scholastic Aptitude Test) or general analogical reasoning ability (which had been measured on the Differential Aptitude Tests) was a better predictor of transfer in their experiment. They found that mathematics ability was a good predictor of transfer, but that there was no relationship at all between analogical reasoning ability and transfer.

This is a perplexing result in that, on the one hand, general analogical reasoning ability is known to be a good predictor of scholastic achievement, but, on the other hand, it was useless at predicting performance in this specific learning situation. Why do the predictions fail?

6.3   Complexity of learning in the classroom situation

Novick and Holyoak explained the failure to find a relationship between analogical reasoning ability and performance in their transfer experiments by suggesting that there is an important difference in the amount of cognitive processing required to solve complex problems in the classroom, as opposed to simple intelligence test analogy problems. As an example of such differences, consider the application process (assuming Sternberg's model of analogical reasoning). In solving an analogy like 'Tall:Short::Wide: ?', the answer can be derived simply by working out the relation 'opposites' between 'Tall' and 'Short' and applying the relation to 'Wide' to generate 'Narrow'. Now, consider again the research by Reed, Dempster and Ettinger (1985), discussed in Part II, on solving mathematics problems by analogy. In that situation, a solution procedure which was useful for solving a problem of a particular type required considerable moulding (i.e. use of the application component) before it could be transformed into a solution to a new problem of the same type. It is this difference in the level of complexity of the component processes in the two different situations that is thought to account for the failure of analogical reasoning to predict performance on more 'computational' tasks.

In ordinary academic problem-solving situations, where students are given an opportunity to learn from examples, they twist and mould the format of *example problem : example solution :: exercise problem : ? exercise solution* (i.e. A:B::C:?D, where A=example problem, B=example solution, C=exercise problem, and ?D=exercise solution) to fit in with their own purposes and their own misconceptions (Anderson and Pirolli, 1984; Kahney and Eisenstadt, 1981; Kahney, 1982). When students are given the opportunity to learn from textbook examples, many turn to an example solution (the B term) as a framework for both understanding and solving their exercise problem, often without reference to the statement of the example problem in the textbook (the A term). It is not surprising that many students fail to induce a schema for problems of a particular type if they don't consider the example and exercise problems (A and C terms) together at some point in their exercise work. Indeed, they sometimes fail to understand what problem is being solved by the example solution, since they often don't even go back to the statement of the example problem to see what the solution they are copying is meant to achieve (Keane, Kahney and Brayshaw, 1989).

Another problem that needs to be tackled is the construction of tests that measure inductive ability. As Whiteley's and Bejar *et al.*'s research shows, what is actually being measured depends to some extent on the type of relation used in test items. As a result, it is hard to say exactly what it is that is being measured with the current crop of tests. Test designers need to develop metrics that will specify the level of difficulty of different test problems. We need to be able to say how and why one problem is more difficult than another. If a problem has one solution alternative that 'stands out' from the others in some way, then it will be an easier problem than one in which all the solution alternatives are related in such a way as to make it very difficult to determine which alternative is the correct one. Some research in this area has already been conducted by Bejar, Chaffin and Embretson (1991), but considerably more will need to be done in the future.

Part III   The Experimental Analysis of Analogical Reasoning

6.4   The importance of knowledge in analogical reasoning and analogical problem solving

Piaget proposed four stages of cognitive development: (1) sensori-motor (age 0–2); (2) pre-operational (age 2–7); (3) concrete operational (age 7–11); and (4) formal operational (age 12–adulthood). Piaget argued that reasoning ability *develops* over time and that mature analogical reasoning is not seen before the stage of formal operations. According to Piaget, ability to think in terms of second order relations, an ability which we have seen is the key ability in analogical reasoning, is not available until the final (formal operations) stage of development. This hypothesis has been tested by research on young children by Sternberg and Nigro (1980). The main finding of interest here was that, prior to the stage of formal operations, children often solved analogy problems by selecting the solution term that is a close verbal associate of the C term of the analogy, ignoring the A:B relation altogether. For example, given the analogy 'Bird is to Nest as Dog is to (a) Doghouse (b) Bone', young children would select option (b) as the solution because of the close association between 'Dog' and 'Bone', which is to ignore the relation between 'Bird' and 'Nest' and its application to the C term. The research thus provides some support for Piaget's theory.

However, Goswami and Brown (1989; 1990) have reported interesting research that casts doubt on Piaget's claim that children can't reason analogically before the stage of formal operations. Goswami and Brown argue that Sternberg and Nigro failed to perform a genuine test of the hypothesis because their test items embodied second order relations that very young children don't really understand. As an example, consider the following problem and work out the second order relation for yourself — Bicycle:Handlebars::Ship: ? The second order relation is 'method of steering', a relation that very young children may not know about. Goswami and Brown pointed to research that showed that children as young as 3 were able to understand and reason about certain causal relations, like melt, cut, wet, burn, open, break, dirty and switch on (electricity), and argued that analogical reasoning research with children should use such causal relations in order to determine whether or not children could reason about second order relations. In one set of experiments they presented 3-, 4-, and 6-year-olds with analogies (in picture format, of course, since most 3- and 4-year-olds couldn't be expected to read) such as 'playdoh : cut playdoh :: apple: (a) ball (b) banana (c) cut apple (d) bruised apple (e) cut bread'. The five completion terms for all the problems they presented were chosen to provide the following options:

1 the correct object and the correct physical change (i.e. cut apple in the example problem);

2 the wrong object and the correct physical change (cut bread);
3 the correct object and the wrong physical change (bruised apple);
4 a mere appearance match for the C term (ball); and
5 a semantic associate of the C term (banana).

Their results confirmed that children as young as 3 are able to reason analogically if they are given problems utilizing causal relations that they understand. Without the relevant knowledge of objects and relations, the children cannot apply their analogical reasoning ability.

In other research with young children, Alexander, Willson, White, Fuqua, Clark, Wilson and Kulikowich (1989) trained 4- and 5-year-olds in the component processes of analogical reasoning. The children were chosen on the basis of their scores on the Geometric Analogies Test — if they did poorly enough to be classified as non-analogical reasoners, they qualified as subjects. Twenty non-analogical reasoners were given the training, and a control group of twenty non-analogical reasoners were given no training. After training the experimental group not only performed better than the untrained group but as well as children who were classified as analogical reasoners.

The research reported by Goswami and Brown points to analogical reasoning ability as a set of processes that are available to people from the age of 3 onwards, albeit to different extents across individuals. The research of Goswami and Brown also demonstrates the importance of *knowledge* as a determining factor in analogical reasoning. People need a lot of knowledge to solve many analogies, just as they need a lot of knowledge in order to solve physics or chess problems, as we have already shown in Part II of this book. However, the research carried out by Alexander *et al.* (1989) shows that analogical reasoning *processes* are also important as they can be trained, and training results in significant improvement in performance.

At the present time the research program outlined by Pellegrino and Glaser has been neither a complete success nor a complete failure. It has not yet fully achieved the goal of understanding in detail the processes underlying test performance on a wide range of abilities, on the one hand, and performance on more complex, real-world tasks on the other. We have names for the processes, but only an impoverished understanding of the 'inner workings' of the processes which have been named. Only when a much deeper understanding has been achieved will the goal of training intelligence be a real possibility, or really be put to the test. The difficulty in understanding performance in the two areas of concern is not a problem simply for the componential analysts, but for cognitive psychologists generally. Every advance in understanding perception, memory, language and problem solving will feed into endeavours to help people become better problem solvers.

Overview

In this overview I would like to draw out some of the main implications of the research discussed in the book. I shall confine my discussion to three topics: the implications of research on learning for the basis of analogical problem solving, search in problem spaces, and individual differences in problem solving and reasoning.

Analogical problem solving and learning

The book began with a review of research on human problem solving on a number of very simple, puzzle-like transformation problems such as the Towers of Hanoi. The research on transfer of learning discussed in Part I revealed that people may experience considerable difficulty in transferring what they know about solving a problem of a particular type when they are confronted with a new problem of the same type. The research showed that subjects sometimes had to be told the relationship between two problems before they could apply previously acquired knowledge in solving a new problem, and even then previous experience was no help if the new problem was more complex than the earlier one.

Another way of conceptualizing the problem of transfer between problems is to ask whether people can see the analogies between similar problems and can exploit these to solve novel problems.

In Part II we found conflicting evidence about people's ability to exploit analogies between similar problems. On the one hand, Gick and Holyoak's research on the radiation problem indicates that people are unlikely to use a prior analogy (the fortress problem) unless they are given a hint to do so. Nevertheless, they are quite successful at using analogies once the idea has been suggested to them. On the other hand, the results of experiments conducted by Reed, Dempster and Ettinger on students' ability to use worked-out solutions of algebra problems suggest that people may experience considerable difficulty in applying analogies in more realistic, classroom situations. Taken together, the findings indicate that people are rather poor at transferring knowledge from one situation to another without considerable guidance. This conclusion is supported by the results of research reported in Part II in which it was shown that experimental subjects were unlikely to construct an abstract schema for similar problems unless they were presented with at least a couple of closely related problems, and provided with information on the principle that united them.

All this has considerable implications for learning, since most teaching is based on the notion that students can learn to extract general principles from problem-solving experiences which they can apply to solve other similar problems.

So, what can we learn from problem-solving research about how to design teaching materials? Textbooks on subjects such as mathematics, physics or computer programming usually contain a number of main sections in which principles are defined and discussed. Principles are sometimes illustrated with a worked-out example. Students are then presented with a number of practice problems which are designed to provide the student with the know-how to apply the principles to all problems of that type.

Research into analogical problem solving, though, suggests that the relationship between the original worked-out example and the exercise problems should not be left to students to puzzle out for themselves, but should be made explicit. Although this might seem just plain common sense, the fact is that many textbook writers do not employ such principles. For example, I know of one standard textbook on computer programming in which exercise problems bear only the most tenuous relationship with the worked-out examples used for teaching purposes in earlier parts of the text. When considering an example situation closer at hand, students often find it difficult to fit worked examples of statistical tests to the data analysis they are currently handling, even when the worked examples are extremely detailed.

Search in problem spaces

In Part I the notion of state space analysis was introduced. This is a method for setting out all possible moves allowed by the rules of a problem. Finding the solution to a problem can be defined as discovering an appropriate path through the possible moves. Such an objective analysis of the overall structure of a problem is only possible for puzzles with a limited number of set moves which can be defined beforehand. For most real-life problems it would be impossible to list a set of predefined possible moves. Moreover, even with puzzle problems, novices are unlikely to appreciate the overall structure of the problem. Simon's model, introduced in Part I, is concerned with the *mental* problem spaces which are extracted from people's personal understanding of a problem; and also with the limitations on problem solving as a result of short-term memory limitations.

According to the information-processing model, people proceed in solving such problems by making local decisions, based on means-ends analysis. People are unable to plan a sequence of moves on transformation puzzle problems because they begin with a limited understanding of the structure of the problem and because working memory capacity is insufficient to hold all the information necessary for forward planning. People often get lost in such problems because the means-ends strategy of evaluating distance from the goal leads them away from the solution at certain critical points in the problem (Atwood and Polson, 1976).

Anzai and Simon (1979) have demonstrated how relatively weak strategies, such as avoiding return to previous states of a problem, could be very useful in understanding and solving problems for which no guidance is provided. In essence, they show how initial attempts at solving the Towers of Hanoi problem could be viewed as a kind of 'exploration' of the problem space. During this exploration, a solver might learn to identify moves that lead to dead-ends, and so to avoid such moves on subsequent attempts at the problem. Avoiding bad moves considerably reduces the size of the problem space. The effect of a reduced problem space would be to make it more likely that a solver will see what leads to what on paths near to the optimal solution path of a problem. Discovering what leads to what makes it more likely that solvers will be able to identify useful sub-goals in solving a problem. If a solver can devise a plan for achieving sub-goals on the next attempt, the problem space might be even further reduced. In other words, initial attempts at solving a problem may set up the conditions for applying more powerful heuristics, such as means-ends analysis, on subsequent attempts at the problem.

The analysis is interesting because we can see how it relates to problem solving and learning in more realistic task environments. If you watch novice students trying to solve problems in domains such as computer programming or mathematics, you will often see them selecting operators almost at random. The student may make ten attempts at solving a problem, 'getting nowhere fast'. But with enough persistence, the student may find a solution, perhaps without understanding it, simply by a process of elimination of operators that led nowhere on previous attempts at the problem. As Simon points out, having a solution to a problem, even a solution that is achieved without understanding while the problem is being solved, provides a basis for further learning. In the Towers of Hanoi problem, knowing the solution to the problem provides the subject with a 'worked-out example' of how the problem could be solved. The worked-out example then serves as a basis for further understanding of the problem.

Novices and experts

In Part II we discussed research on learning in a variety of domains, such as computer programming, physics and mathematics. These were described as semantically rich, formal domains. We saw that in every case experts differed from novices not only in the amount of domain-specific knowledge they had acquired, but also in the way their knowledge was organized and used. We presented ACT*, the cognitive learning theory developed by John Anderson, which attempts to explain procedural learning as the proceduralization of declarative knowledge through practice at solving problems. ACT* also contains mechanisms such as composition, strengthening, and generalization for combining and tuning the production rules that are acquired through proceduralization.

At the present time, most students learn how to solve domain-related problems efficiently only by devoting hundreds or thousands of hours of their time to solving such problems. Unfortunately, it is often only the 'better' students who benefit from such practice. However, an important 'spin off' of research on novice/expert differences has been the identification of many of the strategies experts use in solving problems in particular domains, and psychologists have begun to explore the possibility that novices might be taught domain-specific problem-solving strategies directly.

The training of intelligence

In Part III we looked at attempts by cognitive psychologists to understand and characterize differences in people's reasoning ability in terms of information-processing models. We began with a discussion of Sternberg's work, which suggested that there were no differences between 'good' and 'poor' reasoners in terms of the strategies they employed in solving analogy problems, but that there were differences between the groups in the amount of time needed to run off particular component processes. An interesting finding was that good solvers spend more time on the encoding component; this extra time spent on encoding is believed to make the operation of the inference, mapping and application components more efficient and effective.

We discussed the development of Sternberg's early work, in particular in the models proposed by Heller, who argued that strategy differences between high and low ability groups would only show up when a wider range of subjects was tested on harder problems than those used in Sternberg's research. Heller proposed two strategies, as embodied in her *conceptual* and *interactive* models of reasoning. Her analysis suggested that people in all ability groups were able to solve problems in terms of the conceptual model, if the problems presented weren't too difficult. Good solvers, however, were more likely to engage in interactive processing on the more difficult problems. Unfortunately, as we have seen, some of Heller's interpretations of her protocol data can be given a different interpretation from hers. Still, model building is an ongoing process and there is no reason to believe that future attempts won't provide us with an even better understanding of analogical reasoning processes.

We also discussed the development of analogical reasoning ability. It looks as though this particular reasoning ability is available from infancy, but that lack of a rich knowledge base restricts its use in both children and adults.

Finally, we looked at the question of the possibility of training intelligence. The goal of many people working within the information-processing paradigm is to 'make people smarter', in some sense of the phrase. The idea, simply put, is to try to figure out how to make 'C' students into 'A' students. That's a worthy goal. But at the moment the goal has not been achieved. In the work of Alexander *et al.* we have some evidence that performances on analogical reasoning test tasks can be improved, but generalization of this improvement to related tasks has not yet been found. However, this current failure is nothing more than a goad to researchers who believe that cognitive performance — intelligence — can be improved if only enough were known about the mechanisms underlying human cerebration. And that's why the work will be carried on into the future. Cognitive psychologists have made considerable contributions to our understanding of problem solving and learning over the past three decades, and all the signs point to further increases in that understanding in the future.

Answers to SAQs

SAQ 1
A minimum of seven moves is necessary for solving the three-ring version of the Towers of Hanoi problem. The moves in moving three rings from Peg A to Peg B are:

small ring from Peg A to Peg B;
medium ring from Peg A to Peg C;
small ring from Peg B to Peg C;
large ring from Peg A to Peg B;
small ring from Peg C to Peg A;
medium ring from Peg C to Peg B;
small ring from Peg A to Peg B.

SAQ 2
(a) Solving a crossword puzzle clue.
   Initial state: a string of empty squares.
   Goal state: the squares filled in with the words indicated by the crossword clues.
(b) Playing noughts and crosses.
   Initial state: a three-by-three matrix of empty cells.
   Goal state: a winning line of noughts or crosses.

SAQ 3
The text points out that the degree to which a problem is considered ill- or well-defined often depends upon the solver's knowledge. People who have done a lot of travelling will have acquired knowledge about appropriate travelling operators and the situations in which they apply. For such people, most travel problems would be pretty well-defined. The less experience a person has with such problems, the more likely it is that the problem will seem ill-defined.

SAQ 4 (see illustration at top of page 150)
(a) From state 3 the graph can be extended by moving the medium-sized ring from Peg A to Peg C.
(b) From state 3 it is possible to reach state 1 (a loop), state 2 and state 5, as indicated by the lines emanating from state 3.

SAQ 5
Initial state: Three people, a Host, a Senior Guest, and a Junior Guest. The Host performs three services for his guests. Each task has a different degree of nobility associated with it. The tasks are stoking the fire (least noble), pouring the tea (medium nobility), and reciting poetry (most noble).

Goal state: The Senior Guest performs all three services for the Host and Junior Guest.

Operators: Host and guests can ask to perform a task currently being performed by any of the others.

Operator restrictions: No one can ask to perform a task which is nobler than any task(s) currently being performed. Only one task may be requested at a time.

SAQ 6
Since the three-task Chinese Tea Ceremony problem and the three-ring Towers of Hanoi problem are completely isomorphic (they have the same state space), they can both be solved in seven moves.

Answers to SAQs

SAQ 4 (see also p. 149)

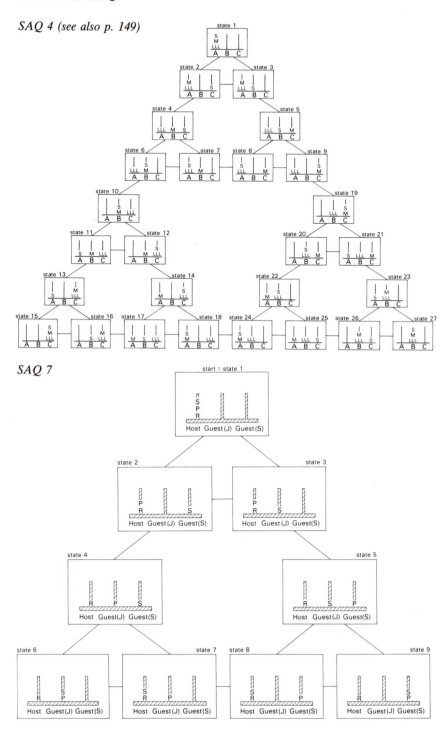

SAQ 7

SAQ 8

The path I take through this state space on the few occasions that I make tea is: state 1, state 2, state 5, state 7 and state 8. Your own path may differ from mine, of course.

SAQ 9

Initial state: General outside fortress with army. Tyrant inside fortress. Roads radiating out from the fortress have been mined. Large bodies of men passing along a road would set off mines, destroying the roads and making them impassable. If the roads are destroyed the tyrant would destroy many villages in retaliation.

Goal: General overthrows tyrant.

Operators: General can use army to attack fortress.

Operator restrictions: General must avoid destruction of army and villages.

SAQ 10

The fortress problem is ill-defined because the operator ('use army') is under-specified. The general's problem is to determine more precisely how the army can be used to achieve the goal, without violating the operator restrictions. The problem is solved when the general transforms the general operator 'use army' into specific actions that can be performed, such as 'divide army', 'send small units along roads', and so on.

SAQ 11

Initial state: Tumour in patient's stomach. Doctor is not allowed to operate. Doctor has special ray which can be used for treatment. High intensity rays destroy healthy tissue as well as tumours. Low intensity rays neither destroy tumours nor damage healthy tissue.

Goal: Doctor destroys tumour.

Operators: Doctor can use special rays to destroy tumour.

Operator restrictions: Doctor must avoid damage to healthy tissue.

SAQ 12

The radiation problem is ill-defined because the operator ('use rays') is under-specified. The doctor's problem is to determine more precisely how the rays can be used to achieve the goal, without violating the operator restrictions. The problem is solved when the doctor transforms the general operator 'use rays' into specific actions that can be performed, such as 'send several low intensity rays from many different directions simultaneously towards the site of the tumour'.

SAQ 13

In Gick and Holyoak's research, subjects who were given a hint that there was a relationship between the radiation problem and the fortress problem performed better than subjects who were not given such a hint. Subjects were also able to use a very general hint about the relationship between the radiation problem and the fortress problem, as shown by the results of the experiment in which the fortress problem story was presented along with two other problem stories that were disanalogous to the radiation problem. In this situation, subjects who were given the general hint produced dispersion solutions to the radiation problem significantly more frequently than subjects who were not given a hint. These findings suggest that inability to notice spontaneously an analogy is the major impediment to analogical problem solving; that applying a known solution in a new problem situation is not a major stumbling block.

However, in the research reported by Reed *et al.* subjects found a hint about the relationship between closely related problems useful only if the second problem was somewhat less complex (measured in terms of the number of possible illegal problem states) than the first problem. This finding suggests that solution processes are as important as noticing processes in analogical problem solving.

Gick and Holyoak point out that the problems used by Reed *et al.* are computational, or multistep problems, and that the solutions to such problems may be difficult to remember. It is also possible that multistep solutions are simply too difficult to apply to new problems because of processing limitations such as limited working-memory capacity.

SAQ 14
(a) I would call the common causal relation something like 'avoidance', since Debbie's goal seems to be to avoid John, and George's goal seems to be to avoid the police.
(b) On a similarity scale of 1 to 10, I would say that on the surface the stories should be given a score of 1, since in the one case we are dealing with a story about a conversation between two women, one of whom later moved out of town, and in the other case a story about a man who seems to decide not to return home while a police car sits in front of his house.
(c) I would give these stories a similarity rating of about 10 on the basis of the causal relation identified in (a). However, if I took other factors into consideration (such as the motives I would attribute to either Debbie or George in wanting to avoid an old flame or ex-husband (my inference), on the one hand, or a jail term (another inference), on the other hand, then I would suggest a lower rating.

SAQ 15
Proceduralization, in this example, would mean that members of the air cabin staff would have to learn how to do things like how to switch off the oven and pull the circuit breaker and devote time to practising the procedures. Strengthening would occur with repeated application of the procedures. Composition would occur, again due to practice, as the staff learned to switch off the oven, pull the circuit breaker, isolate the area and get the fire extinguisher as one smooth sequence of automatic movements requiring no forethought about what needed to be done.

SAQ 16
The domain of the analogy is 'Simon: Information Processing'. The range is 'Skinner:?'. The stem is 'Simon: Information Processing::Skinner:'. The completion term is not given but is represented by the question mark.

The answer is 'Radical Behaviourism'.

SAQ 17
1
(a) Option (c) — Corporal punishment involves beating and capital punishment involves killing.
(b) Option (c) — Noon and eve are both palindromes (i.e. they read alike forwards and backwards). 12–21 and 10–01 are related in the same way.
(c) Option (a) — Yellow and blue are the colours associated with cowardice and gloom respectively.
(d) Evolution.

2 In each of the above cases the second order relation can be said to be the same as the first order relations between the domain and range of each analogy: (a) type of punishment, (b) palindromes, (c) associate, and (d) developed-theory-of.

SAQ 18
This is a particularly interesting protocol, both for the information it contains and for the fact that a lot of information is not there explicitly, but has to be inferred. The relation between the first two terms of the analogy, 'Tell' and 'Listen', can be categorized as a 'contrast' or 'reverse' relation. Although the solver never mentions such a relation, we can infer that 'contrast' (or something like that) is the relation inferred because the first thing the solver says is 'Take', which can be regarded as bearing a contrast relation to the C term, 'Give'. (This is the answer to the second part of the SAQ.)
   This looks like good reasoning — work out a relation between the A and B terms of the problem, apply the relation to the C term in order to generate an ideal solution, and then compare it with the available alternatives for a match or close match (remember the justification component in Sternberg's model). If you look at the solution alternatives again, you'll see that there is one contrast term — 'Get'. This is the correct solution, and the one you'd think the solver would choose on the grounds that get and take are sufficiently close in meaning that 'Get' was more or less the expected solution (this is what justification means in this context). And yet, the solver actually accepts three of the four alternatives as they are presented and finally opts for 'Present' (and note that in this context the solver has presumably adopted the wrong sense of 'Present', taking it to mean 'Gift' rather than thinking of it as a synonym of 'Give'. The reason that the solution is non-analogical is because the subject shows no evidence of trying to match relations between the domain and range of the analogy in making a final selection of a solution.
   Of course, I'm making a lot of inferences here. I'm inferring from the first thing the subject said that the subject was able to work out the appropriate relation between the A and B terms and to apply it to the C term. I'm inferring that the subject was working with the wrong sense of 'Present'. And I'm coming clean about it all in order to give you something to think about when you consider protocol analysis as a method used by psychologists interested in information-processing accounts of cognitive behaviour. A lot of what goes into our final models is based on inferences such as these.

SAQ 19
As already suggested in the discussion of Activity 14, the protocol presented in Section 5.1 does not look like evidence for Heller's models; rather, it looks like evidence for the generate-and-test model of Robert Sternberg.
   The protocol presented in Section 5.2 looks like evidence for the interactive model, even though it's regarded by Heller as a buggy-analogical solution, since the solver uses the relations produced from consideration of the different C and D terms to reconsider the original guess about the ideal solution.
   At the start the protocol in Section 5.3 looks like more evidence for Sternberg's generate-and-test model, rather than for Heller's conceptual model, because the solver immediately produces an ideal completion term—'Take'. But throughout the rest of the protocol there is no evidence that the solver tries to match whatever relations are generated for the C and D terms to the original relation worked out for the A and B terms together, as would be expected under the generate-and-test model.

References

ADELSON, B. (1981) 'Problem solving and the development of abstract categories in programming languages', *Memory and Cognition*, 9, pp.422–33.

ALEXANDER, P.A., WHITE, C.S, HAENSLEY, P.A. and CRIMMINS-JEANES, M. (1987) Training in analogical reasoning', *American Educational Research Journal*, 24, pp.387–404.

ALEXANDER, P.A., WILLSON, V.L., WHITE, C.S, FUQUA, J.D., CLARK, G.D., WILSON, A.F. and KULIKOWICH, J.M. (1989) 'Development of analogical reasoning in 4- and 5-year-old children', *Cognitive Development*, 4, pp.65–88.

ANDERSON, J.R. (1982) 'Acquisition of cognitive skill', *Psychological Review*, 89, pp.369–406.

ANDERSON, J.R. (1983) *The Architecture of Cognition*, Harvard University Press.

ANDERSON, J.R. (1990) *Cognitive Psychology and Its Implications* (3rd edn), W.H. Freeman.

ANDERSON, J.R., FARRELL, R. and SAUERS, R. (1984) 'Learning to program in LISP', *Cognitive Science*, 8, pp.87–129.

ANDERSON, J.R., GREENO, J.G., KLINE, P. and NEVES, D.M. (1981) 'Acquisition of problem-solving skill', in J.R. Anderson, *Cognitive Skills and Their Acquisition*, Lawrence Erlbaum Associates.

ANDERSON, J.R. and PIROLLI, P.L. (1984) 'Spread of activation', *Journal of Experimental Psychology: Learning, Memory and Cognition*, 10, pp.791–8.

ANZAI, Y. and SIMON, H.A. (1979) 'The theory of learning by doing', *Psychological Review*, 86 (2), pp.124–40.

ATWOOD, M.E. and POLSON, P.G. (1976) 'A process model for water jug problems', *Cognitive Psychology*, 8, pp.191–216.

BEJAR, I.I., CHAFFIN, R. and EMBRETSON, S. (1991) *Cognitive and Psychometric Analysis of Analogical Problem Solving*, Springer-Verlag.

BHASKAR, R. and SIMON, H.A. (1977) 'Problem solving in semantically rich domains: an example of engineering thermodynamics', *Cognitive Science*, 1, pp.193–215.

BROWN, E.B. and CLEMENT, J. (1989) 'Overcoming misconceptions via analogical reasoning: abstract transfer versus explanatory model construction', *Instructional Science*, 18, pp.237–61.

CHASE, W.G. and SIMON, H.A. (1973a) 'Perception in chess', *Cognitive Psychology*, 4, pp.55–81.

CHASE, W.G. and SIMON, H.A. (1973b) 'The minds eye in chess', in W.G. Chase (ed.) *Visual Information Processing*, Academic Press.

CHI, M.T.H., FELTOVICH, P.J. and GLASER, R. (1981) 'Categorization and representation of physics problems by experts and novices', *Cognitive Science*, 5, pp.121–52.

COHEN, G., KISS, G. and LE VOI, M. (1993) *Memory: Current Issues*, Open University Press in association with The Open University (Open Guides to Psychology series).

DE GROOT, A.D. (1965) 'Perception and memory versus thought: some old ideas and recent findings', in B. Kleinmuntz (ed.) *Problem Solving*, Riley.

DUNCKER, K. (1945) 'On problem solving', *Psychological Monographs*, 58 (whole no. 270).

ERICSSON, K.A. and SIMON, H.A. (1980) 'Verbal reports as data', *Psychological Review*, 87 (3), pp.215–51.

ESTES, W.K. (ed.) (1978) *Handbook of Learning and Cognition Processes*, Lawrence Erlbaum Associates.

EVANS, J. (1989) *Biases in Human Reasoning, Causes and Consequences*, Lawrence Erlbaum Associates.

GENTNER, D. (1979) 'The role of analogical models in learning scientific topics', Technical Report, Bolt, Beranek and Newman.

GENTNER, D. and GENTNER, D.R. (1980) 'Flowing waters or teeming crowds: mental models of electricity', in D. Gentner and A. Stevens (eds) (1983) *Mental Models*, Lawrence Erlbaum Associates.

GICK, M.L. and HOLYOAK, K.J. (1980) 'Analogical problem solving', *Cognitive Psychology*, 12, pp.306–55.

GICK, M.L. and HOLYOAK, K.J. (1983) 'Schema induction and analogical transfer', *Cognitive Psychology*, 15, pp.1–38.

GOSWAMI, U. (1992) *Analogical Reasoning in Children*, Lawrence Erlbaum Associates.

GOSWAMI, U. and BROWN, A.L. (1989) 'Melting chocolate and melting snowmen: analogical reasoning and causal relations', *Cognition*, 35, pp.69–95.

GOSWAMI, U. and BROWN, A.L. (1990) 'Higher-order structure and relational reasoning: contrasting analogical and thematic relations', *Cognition*, 36, pp.207–26.

GREENE, J. (1986) *Language Understanding: A Cognitive Approach*, Open University Press in association with the Open University (Open Guides to Psychology series).

GREENO, J.G. (1976) 'Indefinite goals in well-structured problems', *Psychological Review*, 83 (6), pp.479–91.

GREENO, J.G. (1978) 'Natures of problem solving abilities', in W.K. Estes (ed.) (1978).

GUILFORD, J.P. (1967) *The Nature of Human Intelligence*, McGraw-Hill.

HAYES, J.R. (1978) *Cognitive Psychology: Thinking and Creating*, The Dorsey Press.

HAYES, J.R. and SIMON, H.A. (1974) 'Understanding written problem instructions', in L.W. Gregg (ed.) *Knowledge and Cognition*, Lawrence Erlbaum Associates.

HELLER, J.I. (1979) *Cognitive Processing in Verbal Analogy Solution*, Ph.D. thesis, Pittsburgh.

KAHNEY, H. (1982) 'An in-depth study of the cognitive behaviour of novice programmers', Human Cognition Research Laboratory, Technical Report No. 5.

KAHNEY, H. and EISENSTADT, M. (1981) 'Programmers' mental models of their programming tasks: the interaction of real-world knowledge and programming knowledge', *Proceedings of the Fourth Annual Cognitive Science Society Conference*, Ann Arbor, Michigan.

References

KEANE, M., KAHNEY, H., and BRAYSHAW, M. (1989) 'Simulating analogical mapping difficulties in recursion problems', in A. G. Cohn (ed.) *Proceedings of the Seventh Conference of the Society for the Study of Artificial Intelligence and Simulation of Behaviour*, Morgan Kaufmann.

KINTSCH, W., MILLER, J.R. and POLSON, P.G. (1984) *Methods and Tactics in Cognitive Science*, Lawrence Erlbaum Associates.

KINTSCH, W. and VAN DIJK, T.A. (1978) 'Toward a model of text comprehension and production', *Psychological Review*, 85, pp.363–94.

KOTOVSKY, K., HAYES, J.R. and SIMON, H.A. (1985) 'Why are some problems hard? Evidence from the Tower of Hanoi', *Cognitive Psychology*, 17, pp.248–94.

LARKIN, J.H. (1981) 'Enriching formal knowledge: a model for learning to solve textbook physics problems', in J. Anderson (ed.) *Cognitive Skills and Their Acquisition*, Lawrence Erlbaum Associates.

LUGER, G.F. and BAUER, M.A. (1978) 'Transfer effects in isomorphic problem situations', *Acta Psychologica*, 42, pp.121–31.

MAYER, R.E. (1983) *Thinking, Problem Solving, Cognition*, W.H. Freeman.

McKEITHEN, K.B., REITMAN, J.S., RUETER, H.H. and HIRTLE, S.C. (1981) 'Knowledge organization and skill differences in computer programmers', *Cognitive Psychology*, 13, pp.307–25.

MILLER, G.A. (1956) 'The magical number seven plus or minus two', *Psychological Review*, 63, pp.81–97.

NEWELL, A., SHAW, J.C. and SIMON, H.A. (1958) 'Elements of a theory of human problem solving', *Psychological Review*, 65, pp.151–66.

NEWELL, A. and SIMON, H.A. (1972) *Human Problem Solving*, Prentice-Hall.

NISBETT, R.E. and WILSON, T.D. (1977) 'Telling more than we can know: verbal reports on mental processes', *Psychological Review*, 84 (3), pp.231–59.

NOVICK, L.R. and HOLYOAK, K.J. (1991) 'Mathematical problem solving by analogy', *Journal of Experimental Psychology: Learning, Memory and Cognition*, 17 (3), pp.398–415.

PELLEGRINO, J.W. and GLASER, R. (1982) 'Analyzing aptitudes for learning: inductive reasoning', in R. Glaser (ed.) *Advances in Instructional Psychology* (vol. 2), Lawrence Erlbaum Associates.

PIROLLI, P.L. (1986) 'A cognitive model and computer tutor for programming recursion', *Human–Computer Interaction*, 2, pp.319–55.

PIROLLI, P.L. and ANDERSON, J.R. (1985) 'The role of learning from examples in the acquisition of recursive programming skills', *Canadian Journal of Psychology*, 39 (2), pp.240–72.

POLSON, P. and JEFFRIES, R. (1982) 'Problem solving as search and understanding', in Sternberg, R.J. (ed.) *Advances in the Psychology of Human Intelligence*, Lawrence Erlbaum Associates.

REED, S.K., DEMPSTER, A. and ETTINGER, M. (1985) 'Usefulness of analogous solutions for solving algebra word problems', *Journal of Experimental Psychology: Learning, Memory and Cognition*, 11 (1), pp.106–25.

REED, S.K., ERNST, G.W. and BANERJI, R. (1974) 'The role of analogy in transfer between similar problem states', *Cognitive Psychology*, 6, pp.436–50.

ROTH, I. (1990) *Introduction to Psychology* (vol. 1), Lawrence Erlbaum Associates in association with the Open University.

SCHOENFELD, A.H. (1979) 'Explicit heuristic training as a variable in problem-solving performance', *Journal for Research in Mathematics Education*, 10, pp.173–87.

SIMON, D.P. and SIMON, H.A. (1978) 'Individual differences in solving physics problems', in R.S. Seigler (ed.) *Children's Thinking: What Develops?*, Lawrence Erlbaum Associates.

SIMON, H.A. (1974) 'How big is a chunk?', *Science*, 183, pp.482–8.

SIMON, H.A. (1978) 'Information processing theories of human problem solving', in W.K. Estes (ed.) (1978).

SIMON, H.A. and HAYES, J.R. (1976) 'The understanding process: problem isomorphs', *Cognitive Psychology*, 8, pp.165–90.

SPEARMAN, C. (1923) *The Nature of 'Intelligence' and the Principles of Cognition*, Macmillan.

STERNBERG, R.J. (1977) *Intelligence, Information Processing, and Analogical Reasoning: The Componential Analysis of Human Abilities*, Lawrence Erlbaum Associates.

STERNBERG, R.J. (1984) 'Mechanisms of cognitive development: a componential approach', in Sternberg, R.J. (ed.) *Mechanisms of Cognitive Development*, W.H. Freeman.

STERNBERG, R.J. (1986) *Intelligence Applied: Understanding and Increasing Your Intellectual Skills*, Harcourt Brace Jovanovich.

STERNBERG, R.J. and GARDNER, M.K. (1980) 'A componential interpretation of the general factor in human intelligence', in Eysenck, H. (ed.) *A Model for Intelligence*, Springer Verlag.

STERNBERG, R.J. and NIGRO, G. (1980) 'Developmental patterns in the solution of verbal analogies', *Child Development*, 51, p.27–38.

WHITELEY, S.E. (1976) 'Solving verbal analogies: some cognitive components of intelligence test items', *Journal of Educational Psychology*, 68, pp.234–42.

WHITELEY, S.E. and DAWIS, R.V. (1974) 'Effects of cognitive intervention on latent ability measured from analogy items', *Journal of Educational Psychology*, 66, pp.710–17.

Index of Authors

158

Pellegrino, J.W. and Glaser, R. (1982) 103, 128, 129, 138, 139
Pirolli, P.L. (1986) 78
Pirolli, P.L. and Anderson, J.R. (1985) 95
Polson, P. and Jeffries, R. (1982) 50

Reed, S.K., Dempster, A. and Ettinger, M. (1985) 79, 141
Reed, S.K., Ernst, G.W. and Banerji, R. (1974) 31, 38, 39
Roth, I. (1990) 101

Schoenfeld, A.H. (1979) 100
Simon, D.P. and Simon, H.A. (1978) 90

Simon, H.A. (1974) 43
Simon, H.A. (1978) 16, 18, 35, 41
Simon, H.A. and Hayes, J.R. (1976) 36
Spearman, C. (1923) 102, 113
Sternberg, R.J. (1977) 113, 117
Sternberg, R.J. (1984) 139
Sternberg, R.J. (1986) 139
Sternberg, R.J. and Gardner, M.K. (1980) 138
Sternberg, R.J. and Nigro, G. (1980) 142

Whiteley, S.E. (1976) 128, 129, 130
Whiteley, S.E. and Dawis, R.V. (1974) 128

Index of Concepts